T0168250

OLDHAM ATHLETIC
Miscellany

*Latics Trivia,
History, Facts & Stats*

DAVE MOORE

OLDHAM ATHLETIC
Miscellany

All statistics, facts and figures are correct as of 1st August 2009

© Dave Moore

Dave Moore has asserted his rights in accordance with the Copyright, Designs and Patents Act 1988 to be identified as the author of this work.

Published By:
Pitch Publishing (Brighton) Ltd
A2 Yeoman Gate
Yeoman Way
Durrington
BN13 3QZ

Email: info@pitchpublishing.co.uk
Web: www.pitchpublishing.co.uk

First published 2009

A catalogue record for this book is available from the British Library.

10-digit ISBN: 1-9054113-9-1
13-digit ISBN: 978-1-9054113-9-9

Printed and bound in Great Britain by Cromwell Press

This book is dedicated to mates, without whom
watching the Latics would not be the same.

Dave Moore

FOREWORD

"That's The One!" That was the phrase in 2003 that I will always remember Simon Blitz exclaiming to myself and our partner Danny Gazal. We always had, and still have, a fascination with football, particularly in the lower leagues and when Oldham Athletic was put into administration we were determined to rescue it and make it a great club again. After all, we were three relatively bright guys – how difficult could it be?

Let me answer that right away. Nothing that we have ever tackled has been as hard and as challenging. There can be no other business in the world with all the nuances of running a football club. The fans, the managers, the finances, the weather, promotion, relegation, players, cup games and hundreds of other seemingly trivial matters all combine to create unbelievable highs and many lows that are associated with clubs up and down the land.

Along the way we have met many tremendous characters, from individual fans who live and breathe the club to perhaps the nicest guy I have met in the game, Big Joe Royle. How fortunate we were that he agreed to help us out for the last nine games of the 2008/09 season. What a legend! Our chief executive Alan Hardy (who we have persuaded that he does not need to wear a tie every day) and the rest of the staff, some such as 'Big Gordon' who have been at the club from the early days to the Premiership and back again, make a great team – and what a team.

Dave Moore had been into my office to interview me regarding his second book *Oldham Athletic Miscellany* and many of the challenges that I mentioned above are recounted in this book. It is a most appropriate follow up to *Oldham Athletic On This Day* which was more of a factual nature so I was delighted to be able to contribute to his next venture.

Perhaps the question we get asked most is, "How can you own and run a club you never supported?"

Well the answer to that is one that Danny first used and one that I now

7

give. It's a bit like your wife – very few people fall in love at first sight (that's just a romantic notion) when you meet. You like, you take the plunge and over time you fall in love and then you can't be without. Well it's no different for us. We have fallen in love and although nothing is forever, Oldham Athletic Football Club is a huge part of our lives. The town and people of Oldham are also very special to us (even some of the councillors). Is it hard, and at times excruciatingly painful?

Yes. Would we change a thing? No chance! Keep the faith.

Simon Corney, Managing Director
Oldham Athletic

INTRODUCTION

My memory seems to recollect that Gillingham could have been my first game but it could just have well been an earlier game in the season. My loyalties were divided between the Latics and Oldham Rugby and every alternate week I used to dash up to Watersheddings to try to get into the "threepenny rush". I was an avid autograph collector and still cherish those scrawly signatures collected so many years ago. It must have been the smell of the Wintergreen that permeated from the dressing rooms that finally hooked me. The smell today still conjures up images, and the memories will remain forever.

I have been fortunate to have experienced watching Athletic playing at the highest level but I have also had to contend with the embarrassment of watching my team having to go cap-in-hand for re-election to the league. I have witnessed three promotions but I have also had to suffer the ignominy of too many relegations. My first visit to Wembley, to watch the League Cup final against Nottingham Forest, is another recollection that will prevail for life.

Oldham Athletic Miscellany is a compilation of a wide range of happenings that have occurred during the life of Oldham Athletic and their fledgling club, Pine Villa. It has not been an easy task, but it has been an exciting time compiling the narrative which chronicles many of the events that have contributed to make Oldham Athletic what it is today – a friendly, homely club.

I sincerely hope that you enjoy reading *Oldham Athletic Miscellany*, and that you will find the content rewarding. I enjoyed the experience of writing the book and hope that you can take some knowledge and humour from reading it.

Dave Moore, August 2009

ACKNOWLEDGEMENTS

I would like to thank the following for their assistance and encouragement in writing *Oldham Athletic Miscellany*. Sincere thanks go to all my team-mates at Surrey Classics Football Club for all their support during my literary ventures. I am indebted to my editor Dan Tester for his patience.

Garth Dykes: *Oldham Athletic Complete Record 1899-1988, The Legends of Oldham Athletic* and *The Who's Who of Oldham Athletic* have been invaluable, as have Stewart W. Beckett: *The Team From A Town Of Chimneys* and *Keeping The Dream Alive* and John Hooper: *An Illustrated History of Oldham's Railways*. I wish to extend my thanks to the *Oldham Evening Chronicle* as well as the websites of Oldham Athletic (official), Oldham Athletic Mad, BanglaFootball.net, Latics Supporters' Club, Canada and Museum de Latique which have all been used for research.

Chief executive Alan Hardy has assisted with all my requests and managing director Simon Corney and chairman Simon Blitz have also made themselves available, when required, for which I extend my gratitude. Rick Holden for his inside information and his permission to use some of the content from his first book *It's A Minging Life* which is still to be published. Ex-players Andy Barlow, Carlo Corazzin, Dave Hodkinson and Dick Mulvaney have also contributed with stories of their escapades in and around Boundary Park and thanks also go to Richie Mulvaney and Steven Chaytor, sons of Dick Mulvaney and Kenny Chaytor.

I wish to acknowledge the contributions of Andrew Bottomley and Paul Prendergast as well as my granddaughter Megan Moore-LaCoste for her speedy touch typing. Thanks also go to Cre8ors Caricatures (cre8orscaricatures.com) who donated the caricature of Joe Royle. A special mention goes to my wife Sandra for her encouragement.

My sincere gratitude goes to each and every one of you.

ABBREVIATIONS

AMC	Associate Members Cup
D1	Division One
D2	Division Two
D3	Division Three
D3(N)	Division Three North
FA	Football Association
FAC	FA Cup
FL	Football League
FLC	Football League Championship
FMC	Full Members Cup
IL	Irish League
L1	League One
L2	League Two
LC	League Cup
LCB	Lancs Combination B
LSPT	Lancs Section Principal Tournament
MA	Manchester Alliance
MJC	Manchester Junior Cup
ML	Manchester League
NL	Non-league
PL	Premier League
SL	Scottish League
U-16	Under-16
U-19	Under-19
U-21	Under-21
U-23	Under 23
WL	Welsh League

AND IT CAME TO PASS…

…that a football team was formed. And the name of the football team was to be Pine Villa. The name Villa was probably taken from the admiration of Aston Villa who had just won the league and cup double in 1894. Pine Villa was formed as an Association Football Club in 1895. The team was to play at the Pine Mill, hence the name Pine Villa. On July 4th 1899, at the Black Cow Inn on Burnley Lane, a meeting took place and Oldham Athletic Association Football Club was born, thus superseding Pine Villa. The new club applied to join the Manchester Alliance League and formed a good squad of amateur players who went from strength to strength. The new team took possession of the bankrupt Oldham County's old ground, the name of which was Oldham Athletic Grounds, hence the name Oldham Athletic. The Boundary Park ground is where Athletic remain to this day. The rest, as they say, is history.

FAMOUS PLAYERS AND SUPPORTERS

Actress Dora Brian's husband, Bill Lawton made his debut for Athletic on September 9th 1946 in a 3-2 win at Rochdale. On August 2nd 1975, locally-based comedian and TV and film star, Eric Sykes was invited to join the board. After missing several meetings, Eric had to resign his position because of his inability to take an active part in the affairs and running of the club. His letter of resignation was accepted on August 16th 1977. Tommy Cannon and Bobby Ball both used to support Oldham Athletic as youngsters. The comedy duo recorded the Wembley song with the team after they reached the 1990 League Cup final. Paul Scholes, Manchester United and England international footballer is a regular visitor to Boundary Park and can often be seen watching games with his son. It is constantly rumoured that Scholes will conclude his playing career at Boundary Park. Page Three stunner and glamour model Michelle Marsh was also a regular visitor to the club especially when her boyfriend Will Haining was playing. Michelle also did some promotional work for the team. Alex Carter, TV star from *Hollyoaks* and Graham Lambert of the Inspiral Carpets, an Oldham-based indie band, is also a long-time supporter. Local veteran cricketer Cec Wright is also an avid Latics fan.

CLUB BOUGHT FOR £1

The 2003/04 season began with Oldham fans not knowing whether their club would be able to complete the season due to the financial problems left by the unexpected departure of chairman Chris Moore. The lack of funding was combined with a distinct threat of relegation due to the loss of most of the previous season's key players. The club found its way into the ownership of marketing manager Sean Jarvis and club accountant Neil Joy who purchased the club for £1 in an effort to keep it running. It was an interim success as the club was later purchased by the Three Amigos – Danny Gazal, Simon Blitz and Simon Corney – who went on to give the club some stability as well as ensuring that Oldham Athletic would indeed survive.

THE COST OF RELEGATION

When Athletic dropped out of the Premiership in 1994 club chairman Ian Stott emphasised the financial importance of getting the club immediately back into the top flight. With a loss of £1.5 million at stake the chairman explained that standard payment, TV appearances and final placement money losses would leave Athletic seriously short of income. At the time, Athletic were carrying a huge wage bill that was geared for the Premiership. The Premiership gave the relegated clubs figures of between £500,000 and £600,000 to help cushion the blow and with the outgoing of players of the calibre of Roger Palmer, Neil McDonald and Tore Pederson, Athletic had trimmed their wages bill considerably. Some of their better players needed to be kept to consolidate the push to get promoted at the first attempt and the FA also helped by chipping in with a financial boost to the coffers. The following season Middlesbrough won the league and Bolton Wanderers were also promoted but the Latics only finished the season in 14th place – hardly what they expected. The free-fall continued with an 18th place finish for the 1995/96 season and the following year they slumped to relegation along with Grimsby Town and Southend United. The club have remained at level three ever since…

PRETTY IN PINK

Athletic made a piece of history on March 2nd 2009 when they became the first football team to completely change their home strip for a league game in order to support a charitable cause. They entertained Leeds United in a game televised by Sky TV sporting a dazzling neon pink strip which was specially designed for the Victoria Breast Unit at The Royal Oldham Hospital. The Latics' official strip manufacturer Carbrini made a one-off set for the occasion as well as a specially branded warm-up shirt. The Victoria Unit needed to raise £250,000 for additions. In a promotional campaign called Link 4 Pink, volunteers made a bucket collection at the turnstiles and after the game all the shirts were auctioned off with the proceeds donated to the cause. The shirt sale raised just short of a staggering £7,000, which swelled the amount collected. The match itself resulted in a 1-1 draw in front of 7,835 supporters. Lee Hughes put the 'Boys in Pink' ahead in the 51st minute but Leeds were level within two minutes after Luciano Becchio headed in a corner kick – and that's how it stayed. The real winner on the night was the Breast Unit.

OUT OF THE CUPBOARD

Manager Mick Wadsworth decided that he had too many players and needed to make some room in the salary budget. In order to do this, he needed to move a player or two out and he called Carlo Corazzin into his office for a meeting. Carlo had heard he'd been put on the transfer list and he went in for the meeting, along with his wife, the day after hearing. He asked Mick why he had been put on the list and the manager explained that he thought that Carlo was an asset he could probably move! Then he pointed to a cupboard in his office and told Carlo and his wife, "There are so many players at this club at this particular time that if I opened that cupboard door, I'm certain that a player would fall out!"

PROFESSIONAL STATUS

When Athletic changed their amateur status in the 1905/06 season the club became known as Oldham Athletic AFC Ltd. They began the new club with a capital of £2,000 which was divided up into 10s shares.

OAFC: PRETTY IN PINK AGAINST LEEDS ON MARCH 2ND 2009

FOURTH DIVISION RUNNERS-UP

After finishing 12th in the 1960/61 season, the Latics looked forward to the following season with some optimism. Manager Jack Rowley was quoted as saying; "No predictions, that's a fool's game, but I certainly think we have a better chance this season than last. One thing is essential; we must get a good start." With new signings Jim Bowie from Scotland, wing-half Peter McCall recruited from Bristol City and full-back Bill Marshall from Burnley, the team certainly looked more balanced. The pre-season quote from Latics chairman Frank Armitage was "Promotion or bust". Little did he know that it could have really been a huge financial disaster if Athletic were not to gain promotion, and they could have gone under after splashing out £45,000 on new players. The club fulfilled their manager's wish by getting off to a great start, going undefeated in their first eleven games. Their first taste of defeat came not in the league, but in a 7-1 League Cup mauling at Second Division pace-setters Sunderland. They recovered sufficiently to win their next two games. A 2-0 win over Oxford United, and a 1-0 away success at Hartlepools United regained top spot in the Fourth Division. The undoubted highlight of the campaign came in a very cold Boxing Day fixture that was played on a snow covered Boundary Park pitch. With many games postponed, the groundstaff worked wonders to get the field playable – did it pay off? Southport were the visitors and they returned to Haig Lane suffering after Athletic's record league win of 11-0 which also created a record score for the Fourth Division. The flurry off the field was matched with a flurry of goals on it; a goal-fest which was led by a double hat-trick from centre forward Bert Lister. Colin Whittaker also scored a hat-trick and goals from Johnny Colquhoun and Bob Ledger completed the rout. The architect of the win was undoubtedly wee Bobby Johnstone who turned in a virtuoso performance that was a complete pleasure to watch. It was very cruel that the master craftsman couldn't have scored a goal himself on that day. Followed by three more successive wins, the Latics had notched up an amazing 25 goals, with just four goals against, in their last five games. They were eight points clear at the end of January although they had played more games than anyone else in the league, except for tenth-placed Stockport County who had played the same amount. A bad run followed where the Latics failed to win in six outings but they were still four points ahead of Brentford by mid March. Athletic finished the season in style with a 6-1 hammering of already relegated Hartlepools but they still missed out on the championship by finishing runners-up and four points behind champions Brentford. Lister led the goalscoring charts with 33 goals and Ken Branagan, Alan Williams and Colquhoun were ever presents in the team. Amazingly, the Latics fired manager Rowley at the end of the season, some reward after winning promotion! The final league table finished as follows:

	P	W	D	L	F	A	W	D	L	F	A	Pts	GAvg
Brentford	46	18	2	3	59	31	9	6	8	39	33	62	.5312
Oldham Ath	46	18	4	1	65	23	6	7	10	30	37	59	.5833
Crewe Alex.	46	15	4	4	50	21	9	7	7	36	37	59	.4827
Mansfield Town	46	16	4	3	61	20	8	5	10	47	49	57	.5652
Gillingham	46	17	3	3	49	23	5	10	8	22	26	57	.4489
Torquay United	46	14	8	1	45	20	6	8	9	30	36	56	.3392
Rochdale	46	16	6	1	48	21	4	5	14	19	38	51	.1355
Tranmere Rovers	46	15	3	5	57	25	5	7	11	24	42	50	.2089
Barrow	46	14	7	2	52	26	5	5	13	30	54	50	.025
Workington	46	13	4	6	42	20	4	9	10	34	48	47	.1176
Aldershot	46	9	9	5	42	32	6	8	9	31	37	47	.0579
Darlington	46	13	3	7	44	33	6	3	14	28	54	44	.8275
Southport	46	11	9	3	47	35	4	5	14	25	71	44	.6792
York City	46	12	6	5	42	25	4	5	14	25	37	43	.0806
Chesterfield	46	7	10	6	43	29	6	6	11	27	35	42	.0937
Doncaster Rovers	46	9	10	4	36	26	5	4	14	28	51	42	.8311
Exeter City	46	9	6	8	27	32	7	4	12	30	45	42	.7402
Oxford United	46	10	10	3	44	27	3	5	15	26	44	41	.9859
Stockport County	46	9	7	7	34	29	6	4	13	22	41	41	.8
Newport County	46	11	6	6	44	29	3	5	15	32	61	39	.8444
Chester	46	11	5	7	31	23	4	4	15	20	43	39	.7727
Lincoln City	46	11	1	11	48	46	2	8	13	20	43	35	.7640
Bradford City	46	8	5	10	37	40	3	5	15	27	53	32	.6881
Hartlepools Utd	46	5	7	11	33	39	2	4	17	23	65	25	.5384

BEST DEFENDER

Chelsea's Marcel Desailly was named as the best defender that former Latics striker Lee Hughes has ever played against.

ATHLETIC HAVE BEATEN EVERYONE

Athletic are in the enviable position that they have beaten, once or more, every team that they have ever played in the league, or the FA Cup. On the down side, Athletic have never won any away games at Brentford, Charlton Athletic, Chasetown, Coventry City, Glossop North End, Rushden & Diamonds, Scarborough or Tottenham Hotspur.

HIGHEST HOME GATES

Athletic beat Hull City 3-0 in their final Second Division game on April 30th 1910 to secure their first-ever promotion to the First Division. The Boundary Park gate of 29,083 was a record. In the following season, Newcastle United provided the opposition for Oldham's first-ever home game in Division One on September 10th 1910. Around 34,000 fans – still a record to this day at Boundary Park for that level – crammed into the ground to witness the event. In the FA Cup, the Latics recorded their biggest-ever home attendance of 46,471 when they went out of the competition to Sheffield Wednesday in a fourth-round tie on January 25th 1930, an all-time record attendance that remains to this day. A remarkable crowd of 45,120 turned up at Boundary Park to smash the previous best Second Division gate when Blackpool came to town on April 21st 1930. The Seasiders won the game by 2-1 in a match where receipts of £2,458 17s 6d were taken. On April 26th 1949 Hull City visited for a Third Division (North) game and the 35,200 who watched the 1-1 draw also set a new record at that level of play. It was James Hutchinson who got the Athletic goal on the day. In the League Cup, the record was set on February 14th 1990 as 19,263 Wembley-crazed fans witnessed the 6-0 semi-final drubbing of West Ham United, a match that almost guaranteed a final place.

CLUB RECORDS

Most League Points (2 for win) .... 61, Division Three, 1973-74
Most League Points (3 for win) .... 88, Division Two, 1990-91
Most League Goals in Season ....95, Division Four, 1962-63
Most League Goals......................Roger Palmer, 141 between 1980-92
Most Goals in Season .....Tommy Davies, 33 in Division Two, 1936/37

KEN BATES ERA

Ken Bates took over as Athletic chairman in December 1965 and he was introduced as being a wealthy man with his own island. Bates had made his fortune in haulage, quarrying, ready-mixed concrete and dairy farming and came to the club believing that it was worthwhile. He arrived at Boundary Park on his first day in a Rolls Royce and immediately set about trying to make little Oldham Athletic a major force to be reckoned with in the Football League, with a not-too-distant promise of European football. It was never going to be a bed of roses as instant success is always hard to achieve as many other chairmen, past and present, can attest. His introduction to football was soul-destroying at times and he was once quoted as saying; "How would you feel after putting money, time and brainwaves into a club to discover on a Saturday afternoon a paltry crowd of around 5,000, which would be unlikely to meet the wage bill." His promise of European football was never fulfilled and the nearest the team came was a pre-season jaunt to Rhodesia which Bates had mastermined. In February 1966 the chairman decided that he wanted to change the secretary of the club and he walked in to the office of assistant secretary Bernard Halford, threw a big bunch of keys across the office, and exclaimed: "There you are Bernard, it's all yours now." It was the first time that Halford was aware of his promotion. Bates had his allies and his foes and Jimmy Frizzell was one of the former after Bates called him into his office and said; "You know that five-pound loyalty bonus I wouldn't give you, well I think you've had an excellent season." He then handed Frizzell an envelope that contained 50 weeks' bonus at a fiver per week in cash. However, the chairman didn't endear himself to the Latics' fans after he introduced the *Boundary Bulletin*, a wonderful matchday programme/magazine. He then added sixpence to the ground admission price and everybody coming into the ground was given a 'free' copy of the new Bulletin. What really burnt Mr. Bates' boats was the fact that he wrote an article in the *Oldham Chronicle* which referred to the Latics fans as; "The lambs of Sheepfoot Lane." He was never forgiven for that quote and consequently had to make a rapid exit. He went on to spend 21 years at Chelsea after purchasing the club for £1 in 1982.

WE ARE NOT AMUSED

Following the defeat in the League Cup final of 1990 the players were not amused. The club's idea to stop off at a hotel in Northamptonshire was not what the players or management would have wanted, win or lose. It became a disaster with several doors coming off their hinges and with various missiles being thrown. The team ended up back in Oldham at some unearthly hour like 5am. The next morning some players could not even remember how they got home. On the following Tuesday night the team hammered Oxford United 4-1, thanks mainly to a superb Rick Holden hat-trick. The players were still sick inside, though, as it had turned out to be a miserable outcome to the year. Athletic missed out on promotion by finishing eighth but the following year the players made a pact that they would concentrate on the league only, given the outcome of the two cup competitions the previous year. The players were duly told by Joe Royle that they were all at Oldham because there was something wrong with all of them! A year later after Athletic had won at Ipswich to secure promotion the players were treated to a meal in an Indian restaurant back in Oldham. Not wanting to miss the chance of an equaliser, Ian Marshall rounded on Joe and asked him if he thought that there was "anyfing" wrong with us now?

INSPIRED ON THE BEACH

Dick Mulvaney played for the Latics between 1971 and 1974 and was a member of the 1973/74 promotion team. He was initially inspired by an injured footballer on Roker Beach in Sunderland. Dick was about 17, and playing football with two friends. An injured professional came over to the three of them and asked them to cross the ball over to him from both wings so he could practise and train his injured leg. Dick went in goal and his two friends went to either wing. They crossed balls over for quite a while and the footballer hit everyone at Dick in goal. He either hit the ball first time on the volley, or took just one touch then shot. Unfortunately, the footballer never did play professional football again, but did make a reasonable career out of football in management. The man's name was Brian Clough.

FA CUP SEMI-FINAL 1912/13

Ewood Park, Blackburn was the venue for Athletic's first ever FA Cup semi-final which took place on March 29th 1913. The team had reached the semis by beating Bolton Wanderers 2-0, Nottingham Forest 5-1, Manchester United 0-0 – after a replay at Old Trafford 2-1 – and with a 1-0 win at Everton. Their opponents were Aston Villa and the tie brought back unhappy memories of a 7-1 hammering at Villa on Boxing Day. Three special trains were ordered but as the Latics were considered the underdogs not many of the Oldham public decided to go and one of the specials was not even used with the second carrying about 50 passengers. The Blackburn public were not really interested in the game and the minimum admission of one shilling was also responsible for the disappointing gate of 22,616. The game itself was settled by the only goal of the game scored by Stephenson in the 32nd minute. Villa went on to win the cup in a dreary 1-0 game over Sunderland that was witnessed by a 121,000 crowd at Crystal Palace. However, the Latics had finally established themselves as a footballing force and were not disgraced as they came within 90 minutes of their first-ever cup final. The Latics team on the day was: Matthews; Cook; Cope; Moffatt; Toward; Wilson; Tummon; Walters; Gee; Woodger and Donnachie.

RECORD FEES

Aug 1913 ..... Charlie Roberts from Manchester United £1,750
Aug 1972 ..... George McVitie from West Bromwich Albion .. £20,000
Dec 1974 ..... David Holt from Bury *£25,000
Mar 1990 .... Paul Moulden from Bournemouth.................... £225,000
Aug 1990 ..... John Keeley from Brighton & Hove Albion £240,000
Aug 1990 ..... David Currie from Nottingham Forest £460,000
Jul 1991 .... Mike Milligan from Everton £600,000
May 1992 ..... Ian Olney from Aston Villa £750,000

* plus Tony Bailey

Jan 1985 .... Wayne Harrison to Liverpool £250,000
Jun 1997 .... Craig Fleming to Norwich City £600,000
Jun 1990 .... Denis Irwin to Manchester United £625,000
Aug 1990 ..... Mike Milligan to Everton £1,000,000
Feb 1992 ...... Earl Barrett to Aston Villa £1,700,000

KEEPING IT IN THE FAMILY – BROTHERS

Joe and his brother Jack Stafford both represented Pine Villa and Oldham Athletic. Joe signed for Villa in 1895 and is the only player in history to play for Villa and also the Latics as a league club. David Walders helped take Athletic from the Lancashire Combination to the First Division in a remarkable four-year spell back in the 1900s and he was renowned for being the club's first captain as a Football League team. David's brother Jack spent a short period on Athletic's books before moving on to Luton Town. Tommy Broad played for Oldham from 1909 to 1912 and was almost an ever present. His brother James arrived at Boundary Park in 1913 and went on to make a name for himself domestically at Millwall and Stoke City, scoring over 100 league goals, before taking up coaching jobs abroad. Daniel and Fred Hooper were siblings who spent most of their time languishing in the Latics reserve side in the roaring 1920s, although Fred was a big hit when he left Oldham to join his hometown club of Darlington. Alfred and Harold Brown took to the field in the 1920s and 1930s although Harold's main contribution was as a reserve and Mid-Week League player. Matt Gray was with the Blues from 1928 to 1945 and made a total of over 300 appearances. His brother Alfred also signed for the club but never made a senior appearance, although he went on to sample league action with Torquay United and Lincoln City. Harry Travis was a member of Athletic's World War II team and his brother Don had two spells at Boundary Park and went on to notch 62 goals in 118 appearances between 1951 and 1956. Bill and Harold Naylor were another set of brothers that played for the Latics in the 1940s and 1950s. In the 1959/60 season, brothers Stuart and Geoff Richardson both represented Oldham. Stuart played in about half of the fixtures but Geoff was restricted to reserve team football. Paul and Ron Futcher were twins who both played for the Latics in the 1980s although they never took to the same field. Paul's son Ben joined Athletic as a trainee in 1995 and remained until he left to join Stalybridge Celtic in 2001. Steve and Garry Hoolickin were both defenders with the Latics in the 1960s and 1970s. Garry completed over 200 appearances but brother Steve made just eight senior appearances before moving on to Bury where he helped them to promotion from Division Four. Garry's son Anthony also tried his hand as a Latics trainee but never made it as a professional. Ex-Athletic manager John Sheridan was a World Cup star and became part of the Latics folklore with his dedication and leadership on the field and his brother Darren also played with blood and guts after he signed from Wigan Athletic in 2001. Darren (or mini-Shez as the fans dubbed him) was never shy of getting stuck in and became the bane of many a referee. Glynn Snodin came on loan in 1991 and played on a week-to-week basis making just nine appearances and scoring a solitary goal. His brother Ian arrived in 1995 and the former England under-21 and 'B' team player went on to make 58 appearances. Athletic's second set of twins to grace Boundary Park were David and Scott McNiven and they both joined the Latics as trainees in July 1994. David struggled to make the senior squad but did make several appearances from the bench whereas Scott went on to complete more than 250 senior games. Both players moved into non-league circles later in their careers.

BACK FROM THE GRAVE

After the *Oldham Evening Chronicle* had incorrectly revealed that former player Ryszard Kowenicki had died in the 1990s, a communication from a Latics supporter in Poland made interesting reading: "I can be absolutely sure about Richard Kowenicki as I've been talking with him just about 10 days ago. On Saturday 21st October 2000, there was a Jubilee match due to a 90-year anniversary of his former club, Widow Lodz. A great number of former Widzew stars had gone to Lodz (ie. Boniek, Smolarek, Dziekanowski). My friend, who works for a local newspaper, told me that Kowenicki would eventually go to Lodz too." Kowenicki commented, "I am living in Denmark and am in good health". Kowenicki was very amused about the news of his death and said that now he is absolutely sure he will be alive for many years. In Poland they have a superstition that if anyone comes to know about the news of their death from other people they will survive until an old age. One of the local papers published a photo from the game and Kowenicki was on the front row. So true enough, Ryszard Kowenicki is still alive and kicking (pun intended).

GROUNDS FOR PURCHASE

The ground at Boundary Park was bought by Athletic for the princely sum of just £3,000.

BLAIR'S DEBUT CANCELLED

Athletic were informed on August 23rd 1966 by the Football League that Ronnie Blair could not make his debut for the team in the League Cup game at Barrow as his registration had not fulfilled the 14-day qualification period.

RECORD SPOILERS

Rodger Wylde bagged two goals at Rotherham United on October 17th 1981 to inspire Athletic to a 2-1 win thus ending the Millers' 28-game unbeaten home run.

TOAST OF BRUNEI

Nineteen-year-old Latics goalkeeper Ian Gray was sent out on loan in the early 1990s but it was no ordinary loan. The youngster, nicknamed Trigger by his mates, was sent to Brunei to help stem the constant barrage of goals that were being leaked by the sultanate's national team. The sultan was ruled to be the world's richest man but his team had lost every game they had ever played until the arrival of young Ian. Gray played a match against Singapore and he had a stormer. The result was a 0-0 draw and the locals acclaimed the team as national heroes. The owner was so delighted that he laid on a royal night to remember in his palace. The deal came about because manager Joe Royle was helping out his ex-Everton teammate Mike Lyon who was in charge of the Brunei team at the time.

LARGE BREAK

Athletic's centre-forward Frank Large, who signed from Carlisle United for £7,500 in December 1965, received a fractured jaw in the match at Swansea on August 29th 1966.

MOST AWAY POINTS

Athletic established a record for the Third Division when they collected 30 points on their travels in their promotion year of 1973/74. The record was the best-ever under the two points per win rule.

GOING UP

Athletic's Boundary Park ground is the second highest league ground in England. West Bromwich Albion's Hawthorns is 551 feet above sea level while the Latics play at an altitude of 526 feet. If non-league teams were to be included, then the highest football ground in England would be Buxton's Silverlands ground which is more than 1,000 feet above sea level.

MILLSTONES & MILESTONES

In 1899 Pine Villa changed its name to Oldham Athletic and by 1907 Athletic were elected to the Second Division at the expense of bankrupt Port Vale. In 1915, with just two home games to go and just one point needed to be English champions, Oldham blew it and finished in second place, which still remains their highest league place. Athletic were relegated from the First Division after finishing bottom of the table in 1923 but in 1958 a 15th place finish in the Third Division (North) meant that they became founder members of the Fourth Division. On Boxing Day 1962 the Latics achieved their best-ever league win – 11-0 over Southport – and in 1963 they finished runners-up and were promoted to the Third Division. In 1969, a bottom-place finish saw Athletic relegated back to the Fourth Division. A third-place spot in 1971 resulted in promotion. A last-day 0-0 draw at Plymouth Argyle secured the Third Division title for 1973/74 and in 1987 the Latics placed third in the Second Division but they lost out against Leeds United in the play-offs. In 1990 Oldham enjoyed their first appearance at Wembley in the League Cup final and they also reached the FA Cup semi-finals. In 1992, a 2-1 win at Ipswich Town meant top flight football again after a gap of 68 years but in 1997 they lost the FA Cup semi-final and were relegated in the same season. New chairman Chris Moore arrived in 2001 and promised Premiership football within five years but in 2003 the team lost out in the play-offs and the club went into administration. Things took a turn for the better in 2004 when Oldham Athletic (2004) AFC Ltd. was formed after a takeover by three American based businessmen (TTA). In 2007 it was another familiar play-off loss, this time to Blackpool, and in 2008 the new stadium plans were put on hold due to the economic problems in England.

ALL-TIME LEADING GOALSCORER

Roger Palmer signed for Athletic from Manchester City on November 19th 1980. Who would have thought that he could have made such an impact at Boundary Park, or that he would go on to become a cult figure by scoring such an abundance of goals? Palmer had been bought, or was it stolen, for the sum of £70,000 that must be one of the most astute purchases that the club has ever completed. He made his debut against Leyton Orient just three days later in a home match that the Latics lost by 1-0. Palmer opened his scoring account on December 13th 1980 when Athletic won 2-0 away at Notts County. On March 19th 1988, the now prolific striker notched his century of league goals in a 3-1 success at Birmingham City. One of the most significant nights in the history of Oldham Athletic occurred on April 4th 1989 when the Latics entertained Ipswich Town at home in a game that resulted in a 4-0 victory. Palmer found the net twice that night and his first goal beat the previous all-time scoring record of 109 goals that had been held since 1955 by Latics legend Eric Gemmell. Mr. Gemmell was there as a guest of honour to witness the historic moment. Palmer scored hat-tricks against Carlisle United, Shrewsbury Town and Stoke City in the 1987/88 season. He notched another three in a match when Athletic took their goal machine to Manchester City and Palmer showed the Maine Road outfit just what they had missed, with a devastating exhibition of finishing in a 4-1 success for the boys in dark blue. His most successful seasons were 1987/88 and 1989/90, when he hit the magical 20-goal mark in both terms. The last senior goal he scored was on January 15th 1992 in a third round FA Cup game at home to Leyton Orient, the team he had coincidentally made his Latics debut against. Unfortunately, the home side lost 4-2 on the day. Palmer's last first team outing came in a 3-1 home loss to Newcastle United. In total he made 488 starting appearances and played 81 games as substitute. His final goal tally was 159. Roger won a Second Division championship medal in 1990/91 and a League Cup loser's medal in 1990. Since he left the club he has become somewhat of a hermit and has never returned to the ground which brought him such success and gave the Oldham fans such pleasure.

WELCOME TO THE TECHNOLOGICAL 1980s

In October 1981 the club decided to introduce a computer to take over the club's accounting, payroll and ticket printing.

SECOND CHANCE SUCCESS

In the third round of the FA Cup, 1978/79 season, the Latics were drawn away at table-topping Stoke City on a day when only two games survived because of the weather. Leicester, who had their famous bubble, was the other game. On a frozen pitch and going to form, Oldham found themselves 2-0 down at half-time when amazingly the referee abandoned the game. In the Tuesday re-match, Oldham went back to the Potteries and won 1-0. A hat-trick by Alan Young gave the Latics a convincing 3-0 win over Leicester City in the fourth round but they went out to Tottenham Hotspur two days later by a similar 0-1 scoreline.

ST. KITTS & NEVIS TOUR

Athletic broke new ground when they did a tour of Saint Kitts and Nevis in May 1998. Their first game against Trinidad and Tobago was on 23rd and ended in a 1-1 draw. On 26th they beat St. Kitts & Nevis 7-1 and then concluded the tour with another friendly win (4-1) over the hosts on 28th. The final table after the two game round-robin tournament was:

1. Oldham Athletic	P 2	W 1	D 1	L 0	F 8	A 2	Pts. 4
2. Saint Kitts & Nevis	P 2	W 1	D 0	L 1	F 5	A 8	Pts. 3
3. Trinidad & Tobago	P 2	W 0	D 1	L 1	F 2	A 5	Pts. 1

SALE OF THE MONTH?

October and November 1978 were months when several of Athletic's players were wanted by other teams. Wolverhampton Wanderers enquired about Carl Valentine (£100,000), Blackpool wanted Steve Taylor (£80,000), Manchester City were chasing Alan Young (£250,000) and Crystal Palace put in a bid for Keith Hicks (£100,000). Tony Waiters of the Vancouver Whitecaps was interested in the transfer of Les Chapman and Steve Taylor but had not made a firm offer.

DAY IN DAY OUT

David Bright played just 18 games for Athletic but the remarkable thing was that he stayed exactly a year. He signed on March 13th 1969 and left on the same day the following year.

JOHN SHERIDAN

John Sheridan joined Athletic in the 1998/99 season for training after being invited by former team-mate and Oldham manager Andy Ritchie. He had been playing for non-league Doncaster Rovers and jumped at the chance to resurrect his playing career making his debut in the 0-0 draw against Wycombe Wanderers on October 24th. He then signed an 18-month contract and went on to help Athletic narrowly avoid relegation in a season in which he was voted Player of the Year. The following campaign he made 41 appearances, scored with an amazing free kick against Bristol Rovers – which was officially measured at 44.9 yards – and had his contract extended for another 12 months. After being voted Player of the Year for a second consecutive term he revealed plans to start taking his coaching badges and commented; "I'm going to see if coaching is for me. And if it isn't, I'll buy an ice cream van." Season 2000/01 was one of disappointment as Sheridan had to undergo surgery on a troublesome knee that kept him out of the team until December, but his return coincided with an unbeaten run which helped Athletic to their eventual mid-table finish. The following year saw manager Andy Ritchie promote the popular 37-year-old Shez to player-coach and Athletic finished the season in a creditable ninth place. In 2002/03, with Ritchie previously gone, another change brought in Iain Dowie to replace manager Mick Wadsworth. This shuffle allowed Sheridan to be appointed player/assistant youth coach, working under Bill Urmson, and he kicked off the season in his usual position in central midfield. However, Dowie was trying to mould a younger team and introduced a rugged and strict training routine which eventually brought about Sheridan's retirement, and he reluctantly admitted; "It has come sooner than I wanted, but I can't grumble too much. I've had some great experiences." The following season, after Chris Moore's great 'Sale of the Century' on players, Sheridan signed non-contract forms to re-register as a player, even though it was almost 12 months since he had last played. His comeback came on an emotional day at Sheffield Wednesday, where the fans still revere him to this day, and he scored a penalty at the home end. After his non-celebration he was treated to a standing ovation from both sets of fans and he later commented; "It was a dream come true because I'd never been back

as a player. The reception was one of the highlights of my career." After Dowie walked out on the club, Sheridan was named as player/caretaker boss with David Eyres as his number two. After three months he was overlooked for the full-time job and the experienced Brian Talbot took the helm. He became second in command and he declared his second and final retirement after a professional playing career of more than 700 matches. The 2004/05 season had a dreadful start which saw the start of the end for Talbot and Sheridan moved from assistant manager to youth team coach, with Tony Philliskirk taking the role of assistant manager. Talbot left in February and there was tremendous support for Sheridan from the fans but he was again overlooked as Ronnie Moore came in and Shez was offered a 12-month deal as reserve-team manager with responsibilities to help at senior level. Sheridan was also given a benefit match at Boundary Park. The following year Sheridan's reserve side had a great season but he also served his first touchline ban for abusing officials. Athletic's fans, disappointed with the poor style of 'hoof-ball' being produced, put pressure on the club to remove Moore from the manager's job and they were eventually successful. John Sheridan was appointed as the club's eighth permanent manager since the end of Joe Royle's era back in 1994. In his first full season in 2006/07 he made his management debut against his former boss Ronnie Moore's side at Tranmere Rovers which resulted in a 1-0 loss. He took his team to the play-offs but they lost to Blackpool although the successful stint earned the new Latics supremo a new three-year contract. 2007/08 was a yo-yo campaign in which the club lost the services of some key players, notably Chris Porter and Richie Wellens. Combined with a crippling run of injuries it resulted in the Latics finishing in eighth place. There were two outstanding achievements though, as Athletic set a club record of seven consecutive away victories, including an FA Cup giant-killing at Everton. As Shez began the 2008/09 season he confessed; "I'm not daft. This is my third season as manager and I've got to win promotion this time, otherwise I'm in trouble." The season began well enough with the club holding on to a play-off spot for most of the season but it all turned sour. The final nail in the coffin came on March 14th when the Latics suffered a humiliating 6-2 loss at MK Dons, and a day later he was fired and Joe Royle was re-appointed to replace him.

SWEDEN & NORWAY TOUR

The team ventured over the North Sea for their 1993/94 pre-season warm-up games. The first part of the tour took place in Sweden and Athletic got off to a disastrous start on July 21st with a 6-0 hammering at Orebro. The tables turned two days later when the Latics dished out a 6-0 mauling over Mjolby Sodra. Richard Jobson, Neil Tolson, Graeme Sharp, Neil Adams (2) and Mike Bernard did the damage. On July 24th the Latics completed the Swedish part of the tour with a 7-1 victory over Sodra Ving with goals from Adams, Ian Olney (4), a Nordin own goal and an Andy Ritchie strike. The first game in Norway took place on July 26th at Stromgodset and an Olney hat-trick and a lone goal from Mark Brennan gave the visitors a 4-0 success. The Latics lost 2-1 at Hamer Kameratene on July 28th with Olney getting the consolation and the tour was completed on July 29th in Tistedalen when a Sharp goal was enough to see off the opposition.

SAFE

A meeting, chaired by Carl Marsden, was held on February 10th 2001 at The Brook Tavern in Oldham with the aim of assisting Oldham Athletic FC to secure its future existence. A group of about 50 Latics supporters met to discuss ideas. The acronym SAFE (Secure Athletic's Future Existence) was accepted for the group's title. A charter was adopted and the club's finances were put under scrutiny. It was disclosed that Athletic's finances up to the period to May 31st 2000 were in poor shape and although they showed a profit of £95,421 they had sold the freehold land and buildings known as Boundary Park, its main asset, to Hiretarget Ltd. With rent of £240,000 per annum to pay, it left the club in a perilous financial position and hardly likely to survive unless serious backing could be obtained. The sole assets left were the Chapel Road Training Ground, and fixtures and fittings at the club. SAFE decided to approach Oldham Council to find out why they were dragging their feet over the redevelopment of Boundary Park. It was also decided that any money raised would be kept independently of the club plus any financial help offered would have to be used in the specific way that SAFE would discuss with the club.

OLD FRIENDS

Some teams just seem to get paired with league and cup games against Athletic on a regular basis. The following clubs have played Oldham head-to-head in the league or FA Cup on more than 50 separate occasions. The table below shows how the Latics have fared against them over the years.

50	Barrow	W21	L24	D5	F78	A84
50	Leyton Orient	W21	L15	D14	F83	A68
50	Middlesbrough	W21	L20	D9	F72	A64
51	Bristol Rovers	W18	L20	D13	F72	A71
51	Fulham	W18	L21	D12	F62	A70
51	Sheffield United	W12	L29	D10	F63	A92
51	Southport	W23	L19	D9	F98	A72
51	West Bromwich Albion	W18	L16	D17	F58	A54
53	Bolton Wanderers	W14	L26	D13	F68	A96
54	Darlington	W25	L15	D14	F103	A67
54	Mansfield	W25	L15	D14	F94	A74
56	Blackpool	W23	L22	D11	F85	A83
58	Chesterfield	W28	L17	D13	F99	A69
58	York City	W22	L19	D17	F92	A84
59	Stoke City	W27	L17	D15	F79	A69
60	Hartlepool United	W29	L18	D13	F103	A85
60	Millwall	W17	L23	D20	F71	A84
62	Blackburn Rovers	W18	L30	D14	F61	A85
66	Carlisle United	W22	L27	D17	F106	A104
66	Crewe Alexandra	W35	L15	D16	F114	A85
66	Stockport County	W27	L21	D18	F100	A86
69	Grimsby Town	W27	L30	D12	F99	A114
69	Port Vale	W26	L30	D13	F97	A89
71	Wrexham	W23	L28	D20	F122	A123
75	Hull City	W26	L29	D20	F96	A109
76	Tranmere Rovers	W31	L28	D17	F114	A116
77	Barnsley	W30	L25	D22	F99	A100
80	Notts County	W30	L33	D17	F116	A108
96	Bradford City	W37	L29	D30	F143	A122

ERIC GEMMELL

The balding Eric Gemmell was born in Prestwich, Manchester and he cut a fine dash on the field writing himself into Latics folklore with his deadly finishing. His career began as an amateur in 1941 when he signed on the dotted line as a 20-year-old for Manchester United. After his service with the navy the tall but tricky centre-forward made his mark as a professional with the other Manchester team from Maine Road. He joined Athletic in June 1947 and in the league match with Chester City on January 19th 1952, Gemmell performed an incredible feat when he scored seven goals in the 11-2 thrashing of the Cheshire visitors, six of them coming in succession. The feat had not been accomplished since April 1936 when Joe Payne had hit double figures in one match with his ten goals for Luton Town helping to annhialate Bristol Rovers by 12-0 in a Third Division (South) game. There were 13,252 spectators who witnessed the game that was played on the snow-covered Boundary Park pitch and Eric's remarkable performance was enough to warm them up on such a chilly day. The previous week Chester had shocked First Division Chelsea with a 2-2 draw in the third round of the FA Cup at Stamford Bridge and much of the pre-match talk was about that. Chester even took the lead in the game twice before Gemmell took a grip on proceedings. In the following season the Latics won the Third Division (North) championship and Gemmell was the club's leading scorer with 23 goals from only 27 league games as he had suffered through injury. His total included three hat-tricks against Darlington Town, Hartlepools United and Tranmere Rovers. Eric was transferred to Crewe Alexandra in February 1954 and his final league club was Rochdale although he continued turning out in non-league football until 1960 with Buxton, and as a player/manager with Nantile Vale of Wales. In all, he made 274 league appearances scoring 146 goals. His record for Athletic in all competitions was; played 218, scored 120. His aggregate goals total of 109 for the Latics was finally beaten by another Oldham legend, Roger Palmer, on April 4th 1989 when the first of his two goals in a 4-0 victory against Ipswich Town surpassed the record. Eric was at Boundary Park on the night to witness the momentous occasion and he presented Palmer with an inscribed statuette on the field. Eric Gemmell died in Cambridge on February 20th 2008.

RELEGATION

Oldham Athletic have tasted relegation seven times in their Football League history. The first time was in the 1922/23 season when they dropped out of the First Division with Stoke City. The season started off well enough with three wins in the first six games but it started to go wrong in October after the Latics had beaten Chelsea 2-0; they went twenty games with only one victory, a 2-1 success over Preston North End. The run lasted in excess of four months and included two groups of consecutive losses (five and eight) which left the Latics five points from safety. Back-to-back wins over Birmingham City in February gave some hope but only three more wins before the end of the season meant the inevitable. Their second drop came in the 1934/35 campaign when they went down from the Second Division along with Notts County. They won only five games up to the New Year, the best win being 5-0 at home to Hull City. A run of nine consecutive defeats began with a 4-2 loss at Newcastle United on December 15th and when their next win, a 3-1 success over Bradford City in February, arrived they were four points adrift from safety. The club managed just four more wins, including a morale building 7-2 drubbing of Bury, but it wasn't enough to avoid relegation. The 1953/54 season began and the Latics had to wait until September 14th before they enjoyed a victory which came in a drab 1-0 success over Lincoln City. With a dismal total of five wins before January, Athletic were bottom of the pack. Only three more wins were achieved before the end of the season that meant banishment to the Third Division (North). In 1957/58 the Latics won their opening-day fixture 1-0 at home to Carlisle United in front of 11,339 supporters but the fans had to wait until September for the next win which was a 4-0 success over Hartlepools United. By the turn of the year Athletic were in 11th position but the remainder of the campaign was not as fruitful. A 9-0 humiliation at Hull City on April 5th left Athletic in 18th spot in an unusual season where the teams in 13-24th positions would become founder members of the Fourth Division. The remaining fixtures did bring wins, notably a 5-1 home success over Chester City, but the team eventually finished in 15th place and as such were evicted to their new home for the following season. Athletic's fifth relegation occurred in 1968/69. After a 4-0 loss at Luton Town on the opening day of the Third Division season, the Latics achieved one solitary win before November. It was a dreadful run that included seven successive losses and a 6-0 mauling at Brighton & Hove

Albion. Athletic had taken just five points from their opening 16 fixtures and were securely rooted at rock bottom. More heavy losses came: 5-1 at Swindon Town, 5-2 at home to Stockport County and 6-2 at Tranmere Rovers and the Latics were sent down with Crewe Alexandra, Hartlepool and Shrewsbury Town. A successful spell resulted in Athletic reaching the pinnacle of the Premier League but the next relegation came along in the 1993/94 season. With only three league wins before December, the Latics still occupied 18th spot even after they had lost 5-2 at home to Manchester United on December 29th. An undefeated February also allowed the Latics to progress in the FA Cup with cup wins over Stoke City and Barnsley. Athletic lost 3-2 at Old Trafford on April 4th and a week later they played United again in the FA Cup semi-final, eventually capitulating in a replay. The Latics completed the season tired and riddled with injuries. They did not win another game and were demoted along with Sheffield United and Swindon Town. Further displacement occurred in the 1996/97 season when their final demotion was completed. The season could not have started much worse as the players had to wait until October for the first three points that came in a 3-0 home win over Port Vale. The victory still left the team four points away from safety. Two successive 3-0 away wins at Grimsby Town and Bradford City, respectively, lifted spirits a little and the 2-1 win over Manchester City in December raised them out of the bottom three and level on points with the sky blue half of Manchester. The Latics entered the New Year and had to wait until March for the next three-pointer; a 1-0 success at Queens Park Rangers, but it still left them rooted at the bottom. From then on the club won just three more times but the victories brought plenty of goals. They defeated Wolverhampton Wanderers 3-2, Swindon Town 5-1 and won 3-0 over Norwich City in the final game of the season. The wins were not enough to secure safety and the Latics dropped to the third level along with Grimsby Town and Southend United, where they have remained ever since.

SAVED BY GOAL DIFFERENCE

Oldham Athletic avoided being relegated in the inaugural season of the Premier League in the 1992/93 season thanks to a final-day 4-3 victory over Southampton. Crystal Palace were the unfortunate team to go down with 49 points from 42 games, the joint highest total for any team to be relegated from the top division.

ONE-GOAL WONDERS

Ex-Latics striker Jimmy Fryatt is credited as having scored the fastest ever Football League goal when he found the Tranmere net in an officially recorded time of just four seconds when he was playing for Bradford Park Avenue back in 1964. For other players it sometimes takes longer. There are eight Athletic players who have notched over 100 appearances but have only hit the old onion bag once.

Jimmy Hodson	1905-19	289 appearances
Billy Porter	1926-35	284 appearances
Beau Ratcliffe	1935-46	169 appearances
Wilf Hobson	1953-59	180 appearances
Alan Lawson	1964-70	149 appearances
David Holt	1974-80	162 appearances
Paul Futcher	1980-83	113 appearances
Craig Fleming	1991-97	189 appearances

Other players who have never gone beyond a single goal for Athletic are: Rex Adams, Mark Arber, Chris Armstrong, Viv Aston, Tony Bailey, Alan Ball, Colin Barlow, Mark Bonner, Billy Boswell, Billy Broadbent, Harold Brown, George Burrows, Charlie Butler, Bob Carmichael, Laurence Cassidy, Simon Charlton, John Clarke, Paul Clements, Bobby Collins, Billy Cope, Terry Crossley, Dean Crowe, Jack Cutting, Eric Davis, Billy Douglas, Dickie Down, Billy Fergusson, Mike Flynn, Ken Ford, Tony Foster, Vincent Foweather, Steve Gardner, Luigi Glombard, Danny Hall, Tony Hateley, Don Heath, John Heaton, Charles Hemsley, Charlie Hey, Fred Heywood, Clint Hill, Wilf Hobson, Andy Hodkinson, Bill Hooper, Mark Hughes, Alan Hunter, George Hunter, Mark Innes, Harry Jackson, Bob Jackson, Billy Jeavons, Chris Jones, Paul Jones, J. P. Kalala, Glenn Keeley, George King, Bill Lawton, Alf Lee, Derek Lewin, David Livermore, Lourenco, Neil McDonald, Gerry McGowan, Jimmy McIlroy, John Martin, John Mitchell, Maheta Molango, Kevin Moore, Johnny Morrisey, William Murphy, Martin Nuttall, Matt O'Halleran, Toddy Orlygsson, Gareth Owen, Tom Parnaby, Andy Paterson, Jim Pennington, Alan Philpott, Billy Porter, Marc Richards, Jordan Robertson, Jack Scholfield, Robert Scott (1959), Robert 'Rob' Scott (2005), George Shaw, John Shufflebottom,

Nick Sinclair, Peter Skipper, Glynn Snodin, Harry Spink, Stefan Stam, Phil Starbuck, Ernest Steele, Bob Stewart, Paddy Stokes, Ryan Sugden, Robert Tannahill, Ray Treacy, Austin Trippier, Walter Trotter, Albert Valentine, Bill Vallance, Michel Vonk, Wilkin Ward, Paul Wilkinson, Brian Woodall and Fred Worthington.

TWO TIES – 16 GOALS

The 1990 FA Cup semi-finals produced an amazing 16 goals. The matches were Crystal Palace 4-3 Liverpool, and Manchester United 3-3 Oldham Athletic. The United versus Oldham replay was won by United 2-1. There were an astonishing 16 different goalscorers in the two match-ups. The Palace goalscorers were Bright, O'Reilly, Gray and Pardew while the hitmen for the Scousers were Rush, McMahon and Barnes. On the mark for the Reds were Robson, Webb, Wallace, McClair and Robins while the hard-done-by Latics net finders were Barrett, Marshall, Palmer and Ritchie.

COSMETIC SURGERY

Artificial pitches were banned by the English Football Association in 1988 forcing the top two levels of football clubs to instigate the removal of their plastic surfaces. Queens Park Rangers, Luton Town, Oldham Athletic and Preston North End all used artificial turfs. When the Latics finally reached the First Division in 1991 their pitch was ripped up.

LET THERE BE LIGHT

Athletic contested a game under floodlights for the first time at Derby County's Baseball Ground on March 19th 1956, a game which they lost 2-0. The first ever floodlit game at Boundary Park was played on October 3rd 1961. First Division Burnley were the visitors for a friendly game and 15,520 supporters witnessed the game which ended in a 3-3 draw. Each of the four pylons was 115ft high and almost 1½ miles of cabling was used in their construction. Most of the funding came from voluntary donations and John Clayton, who had worked tirelessly in helping the project, did the official turning on of the lights. Bert Lister, Bobby Johnstone and John Liddell scored the Latics goals.

FOOTBALL'S NOT A GAME OF LIFE OR DEATH

When Rick Holden first arrived at Oldham from Watford, he had come from such a harsh management regimen that it made Sparta look like a walk in the park. He was introduced to all the people at the club and then disappeared home ready for his debut away at Blackburn. Just as he was leaving, manager Joe Royle collared him and asked him how he was going to get to the ground the following day? Rick panicked thinking, *"My God, what's this about? Don't they own their own coach?"* It turned out that he was thinking of saving Rick the journey from Skipton to Oldham only to return to Blackburn that was half the distance to Oldham. He couldn't believe this turnaround in management philosophy – until his home debut. When he made his first home appearance the following week against Watford, the club he had left and despised for a few weeks, he was obviously a little apprehensive. In the first minute the ball made its way out to Rick and in front of the home dugout he trod on the ball and fell over. He looked at the bench expecting a few black looks but they were all creased up with laughter. On the bench that night were the subs, the coaches and management, the kit man, the club hairdresser, the club suits emporium guy (Blacky), the tea maker and every other Tom Dick and Harry. Rick quickly realised that this was the place to be. It didn't take life or football too seriously and this was a recipe for success.

CHESHIRE COUNTY LEAGUE

Athletic reserves have spent just one season in the Cheshire County League. It was in the 1945/46 season.

INSIDE OUT SOCKS

Neil Redfearn, the man who will for ever be remembered as the player who scored 'that' penalty that got Oldham promoted back to the First Division after a gap of 68 years, always wore his Oldham socks inside out as a means to prevent the seam rubbing against his foot. However, when the club became more affluent and got better quality socks he continued to do it as a form of superstition.

CAN WE START AGAIN?

Athletic scored two goals but still lost 3-2 at home to Mansfield Town on September 18th 1948. They had then lost seven and drawn one of their first eight matches and had scored just four goals in the process. It was the worst start to a league season ever by any team in the Football League. The team had been riddled by injuries but the introduction of Eric Gemmell in early October was the catalyst for a change in fortunes for the club. His 23 league and cup goals, partnered with Ray Haddington's contribution, gave the striking partners a total of 45 goals for the season, a higher than average total for that division. The Latics finished the season in sixth place, just 10 points behind champions Hull City. If only they had got a good start to the season!

PALMER'S FAREWELL

Athletic entertained Manchester City on May 14th 1991 for all-time leading marksman Roger Palmer's testimonial game. In testament to his popularity, 15,700 fans turned out to see the Latics beat their neighbours 3-2. Gary Flitcroft put the visitors ahead but Richard Jobson levelled the score just before half-time. It was inevitable that Palmer would score and he put the home side ahead with a goal that brought the expected spontaneous "Ooooh, Roger Palmer" chants from the Oldham faithful. Ian Marshall made it 3-1 before Niall Quinn reduced the deficit in what was a very competitive friendly.

TON-UP BOYS

Only three players have scored more than 100 goals for Athletic. Roger Palmer is the all-time leading scorer for the Latics with 157 goals in total, 141 of his strikes coming in the league. Palmer was with Athletic from 1980 until he retired in 1994. The second player to achieve a 'ton' was Eric Gemmell who blasted 120 goals, with 109 of them coming in league games. Gemmell was an Athletic favourite from 1947 until he left to join Crewe Alexandra in 1954. The third member of the '100 club' is Latics legend Andy Ritchie who scored 107 goals, 84 of which were league goals, between 1987 and 1998. His last goal for Athletic came in the 3-0 home win over Wrexham on 27th January 1998.

KEEPING IT IN THE FAMILY – FATHERS AND SONS

Joe Thompson joined the Latics from Chadderton Athletic in the 1905/06 season but played just five Lancashire Combination games. His son Jimmy Thompson (Snr.) played for Oldham in 1920 and his son Jimmy Thompson (Jnr.) followed in his own father's footsteps in the 1950s. Jimmy (Jnr.) Thompson's son Steve Thompson was also on the Latics books as a youngster and he went on to sample league football with Bolton Wanderers. To further the family ties, Jimmy Thompson (Snr.) also had a nephew that played for the Latics called Norman Wood who made just one appearance at Southport on March 4th 1939 – a real family affair. Another 1920s star was Teddy Ivill who spent five seasons at Boundary Park. Teddy's son Jeffrey played as an amateur in the 1940s but never reached first team level. Fred Ogden played in goal for Athletic from 1941 to 1956 and his son Chris followed in his father's footsteps by tending the nets from 1967 to 1978, and aiding the club to a record ten-game winning league sequence. Alan Williams used to strut his stuff in the 1960s and his son Gary also gave sterling service at Boundary Park. Athletic's most consistent performer Ian Wood had a son, Clark, on the Latics books although he never reached senior level. The late Ken Branagan was also a 1960s hero and his son Jim captained the Latics reserve side for many seasons before he went on to establish his own successful career at Blackburn Rovers. At the age of 43 years, Ken played alongside his 18-year-old son in a Cheshire League game back in 1974. George Jones was a member of the 1973/74 team that won the Third Division championship and his son Alex joined Athletic in 1981. Alex found it hard to establish himself in the team and later moved to Preston North End where he helped them to promotion in 1986/87. Tommy Wright was at the club for three spells between 1986 and 2009; he followed in his father Tommy's footsteps, a player who represented the Latics in the 1950s. Tony Philliskirk joined the club in 1988 for a fee of £25,000 and although his first-team chances were limited, he left a good enough impression to return to the club as a coach and assistant manager in 1998, eventually reverting to youth team coach in 1994. His son Danny, a product of Tony's youth team, was snapped up by big spenders Chelsea in 2007 on a lucrative four-year contract.

ISLE OF MAN FOOTBALL FESTIVAL

The Isle of Man Football Festival in 1987 began on July 27th in a game which Athletic came unstuck by a 1-0 scoreline to Dundee. Two days later the Latics notched their first win, a 1-0 success, against Galway. Tony Ellis, one of Joe Royle's first signings, scored the only goal of the game. The final match of the tournament was against Bury on July 30th when both teams fought out a 1-1 tie with Roger Palmer netting for the Blues. There was an unofficial game on the Saturday morning of the final against Hibernian as neither team had made it to the final. The game was played out at the Douglas Bowl and although Hibs beat the Latics 3-0, it was the match when Andy Goram first caught the eye of the Scotsmen.

RACING CERTAINTY FOR A GOAL

All-time record goalscorer Roger Palmer had a strange ritual that he performed before he played any games at Boundary Park. He used to get changed at 2.00pm and then watch the horse-racing on the television until 2.40pm, the time for the team talk.

CONSECUTIVE APPEARANCES

David Wilson was a skilful, reliable and tireless performer who was one of the best-ever half-backs to play for Athletic. He remained at Boundary Park from 1906 until 1921, a remarkable feat in itself. He amassed 368 games for the Latics while scoring 18 goals and he set a Football League record of 264 consecutive appearances with Oldham.

1981/82 WARM-UP GAMES

The first 1981/82 pre-season warm-up game against Coventry City was played at home on August 18th in a match which Athletic won 2-1 with goals from Rodger Wylde and Jim Steel. Everton at home was the next opposition on August 22nd and this game resulted in a 1-1 draw with Steel again on the mark. The final friendly game was played at Rochdale on August 24th but this time the Latics went down 1-0. The cost for the 81/82 friendlies was set at adults £2 seating and £1 standing.

FIRE DELAYS KICK-OFF BUT MCDONALD CHIPS IN

A huge away following went to Goodison Park on January 5th 2008 to see Athletic take on Premiership team Everton in a third round FA Cup game. A fire in a chip shop outside the ground delayed the kick-off by half an hour but it was Athletic, on the back of six successive away wins, who were on fire when play finally started. As expected, Everton dominated the main share of possession but on the stroke of half-time Gary McDonald unleashed a rocket shot to stun the Toffees supporters and give the Latics the shock result of the round in front of 33,086 passionate supporters.

MEAT PIE FRED

Every club has its characters, those supporters who follow their team through thick and thin. One of the most 'famous' supporters of the Latics was the legendary 'Meat Pie Fred'. He was so-called because he would always be seen in the Chaddy End, pie in hand, shouting his heart out for the lads. The following tribute to the late Roland 'Meat Pie Fred' Shaw was first sung on the back of a Barlow's coach on the way to Bristol Rovers in 1976. 'Meat Pie Fred' loved it and would dance along to it. Sadly, characters like Roly are no more as the new fans take over, but you can never take away the memories. Ask anybody who ever witnessed the infamous 'Meat Pie Fred'. Tribute below:

Oh, he's just one of those people who loves eating pies,
When t' chippy's sold out there'll be tears in his eyes,
He'll cause a riot and the windows he'll break,
He won't eat cheese n' onion and definitely not steak,
Cos he's a meat pie fanatic they're his favourite grub,
He'll buy em' from chippy and his local pub,
He'll eat them forever until he dies,
Cos Roland loves eating meat pies!

BEAT US IF YOU CAN

From January 1st 1910 until the end of the season, a total of 22 games, the Latics lost just one match, a 2-0 defeat at Stockport County on March 25th.

PINCH ME SEASON

For those supporters that experienced it – it will remain in their memories for a lifetime. The 1989/90 season was manager Joe Royle's eighth in charge. Optimism was high with a good nucleus of players which included Denis Irwin, Andy Barlow, Earl Barrett, Mike Milligan, Willie Donachie, Andy Ritchie, Ian Marshall, Paul Warhurst, Andy Rhodes and the ever popular Roger Palmer. Royle boosted his squad with the acquisition of Neil Adams from Everton and Rick Holden from Watford. The first few games hardly yielded the points needed to fill the Latics faithful with the desired confidence as they had to wait until the fifth game of the season for their first victory; a 3-2 home success over Plymouth Argyle. The 7-0 thrashing of sorry Scarborough in the League Cup on that magical October night became the catalyst for the season. November came and went with the team unbeaten, the highlight being the 3-1 demolition of league champions and First Division leaders Arsenal in front of almost 15,000 on the artificial turf of Oldham. January became cup month with two games against Birmingham City needed to pass them through the FA Cup third round. Goals from Ritchie and Scott McGarvey put paid to Brighton & Hove Albion in a 2-1 fourth round game and it took a replay, after a remarkable 2-2 game at The Dell, to see off First Division Southampton at Boundary Park in the fifth round. Ritchie and Milligan got the decisive goals in front of almost 19,000 supporters who had packed into the ground. Athletic were making the footballing world look up and were becoming everybody's favourite underdog team, unless of course they were playing your team! Euphoria was surrounding every game with the TV stations eager to cash in on the surprise Second Division club that were knocking out all-comers. Was it possible that little Oldham could be aiming for the treble: promotion, the FA Cup and the League Cup? It was a distinct possibility that they could be visiting Wembley twice, a remarkable feat for a team who had never visited the twin towers before. The first leg in the semi-final of the League Cup was played on 14th February and Athletic all but booked their first London trip with a 6-0 annihilation of West Ham United. February witnessed the marathon fifth round of the FA Cup tie against

Everton who were trying to put a stop to the relentlessly marauding Latics who had shown no respect for any of their opponents, no matter how good their reputation was. The Toffees forced a 2-2 draw at Boundary Park in front of another 19,000-plus gate and the bad tempered replay just four days later ended 0-0 in front of 36,663 fans at Goodison Park. The game went to extra time and Everton old boy Ian Marshall stunned the home crowd by heading the visitors into the lead. It took a late penalty from Kevin Sheedy to save Everton's blushes. Athletic eventually won through to the sixth round after another replay at Boundary Park when 19,346 attendees saw a Palmer strike and a Marshall penalty finally exclude the Toffees from the competition. Just four days later they faced Aston Villa in a quarter-final FA Cup game. True to form the Villans were brushed aside with consummate ease when an astonishing 3-0 win sent the Latics into yet another semi-final! It is reputed that around this time manager Royle went into a local pub and a delirious Latics fan standing at the bar continually kept repeating, "Pinch me!, pinch me!" Hence, the name of the season became known as the 'Pinch Me Season'. Athletic had to meet old foes Manchester United in the semi-final of the FA Cup and what an encounter that turned out to be. The game was played at Maine Road, Manchester and 44,026 turned out to witness an enthralling 3-3 draw in another game that taxed the resolve of Athletic's stamina by going to extra time, yet again. The pace continued to be relentless and just three days later they had to do it all again at the same venue, but this time Mark Robins scored the winner for the Reds to deny Athletic their second Wembley appearance in the same season. The Latics were, by this time, struggling with injuries but their last game in April was one which no player wanted to miss – their first-ever Wembley cup final. Although they went down 1-0 to a Nigel Jemson goal, they had won the hearts of supporters the world over who had witnessed their exploits through the medium of TV. Athletic finished in eighth spot just three points away from the elusive play-off position which they would have probably achieved had it not been for the 19 energy sapping cup ties, many of which went to extra time. In conclusion, they may have won nothing but they had established themselves as a force to be reckoned with, gaining the respect of the TV football-viewing public the world over.

CAN WE USE YOUR WARM PITCH?

Athletic were one of the few teams around in the 1980s to have undersoil heating and some of the bigger teams wanted to keep in trim by taking advantage of the fact. Glasgow Celtic suggested a friendly match at Boundary Park on January 2nd 1982. Oldham agreed to stage the match if Celtic would accept just 50% of the receipts. The match never took place as the Scots had to cancel at short notice. On January 16th 1982, the Latics entertained Manchester United but lost the encounter 3-1, with Paul Heaton getting the Latics goal. United wanted the game as the Old Trafford team did not have the luxury of a heated pitch. Soon-to-be Latics player Scott McGarvey scored a goal for the Reds.

FANS RAISE THE ROOF

Athletic beat play-off hopefuls Middlesbrough by 2-0 at Boundary Park on May 7th 1991. The ground was in an eerie state with work having already commenced on the Chaddy End. The roof was partially removed in preparation for the change over to a 3,200 all-seater stand. With 14,213 fans roaring them on, Ian Marshall and Rick Holden got the goals to see off the visitors.

KEEPING IT IN THE FAMILY

Harry Grundy served the club from 1914 until he retired in 1939. Totally at home in either full-back position, he went on to achieve almost 300 league games for the Latics. His nephew Arthur Grundy signed amateur forms with the club in 1939. Harry Stock was on the Latics' books from 1948 to 1951 and he partnered such illustrious players as Ray Haddington and Eric Gemmell. He made quite a name for himself with some impressive performances as an inside-forward. Aston Villa courted his services but Athletic held onto their prize asset. Unfortunately, his last two seasons were dogged by injury and he was forced to retire from the game. Grandson Paul Warhurst also played for Athletic and he arrived at Boundary Park in 1988 from Manchester City for a fee of £10,000. Paul was a member of the Athletic team that stepped out for their first-ever Wembley appearance in the League Cup final against Nottingham Forest in 1990.

JIMMY FRIZZELL

Jimmy Frizzell was previously a ship's plumber and he joined Athletic from Morton in 1960 for the princely sum of £1,500, a fee that eventually turned out to be a long-term bargain. Little did he realise that his relationship with the Latics would last for 22 years, both as a player and as a manager. He made his debut in a 2-1 loss at home to Northampton Town on a day when goalkeeper Jimmy Rollo and centre-forward Kevin McCurley also played their first games for the Latics. Frizzell was a utility player who was equally comfortable at inside-forward, wing-half or full-back and he went on to make a total of 350 appearances, scoring 58 goals in the process. He took the managerial reins after Jack Rowley was sensationally sacked at the end of 1969 and Frizzell said; "I had been at the club for ten years as a player and I was asked to take over on a caretaker basis when Jack was dismissed. We were in a bit of a mess when I was appointed. In fact, we were heading for re-election at the foot of the Fourth Division. Looking back, I suppose I must have done something right because we ended that season halfway up the table and I was offered the job on a permanent basis." Jimmy's first full season in charge culminated with promotion to the Third Division. It also included a £70,000 windfall to the club from the Ford Sporting League *(qv)* and Jimmy also built a team that went on to achieve promotion to the Second Division as champions in 1973/74, a feat that was finally achieved with a 0-0 draw at Plymouth Argyle. Without doubt, Frizzell had laid a firm foundation for his successful successor Joe Royle, as he had taken the team from the doldrums of being a relegation-haunted club in the Fourth Division to being a well-respected and well-established Second Division outfit. It came as a great shock to the footballing world when the popular Scotsman was sensationally fired in 1982, a dismissal that took him from the role that he ironically entered in a very similar fashion. At the time he left his office, Frizzell was the second longest-serving manager in the entire Football League, second only to the admired Brian Clough. Such was the warmth of the Oldham people towards their 'Sir Jimmy Frizzell' that 2,000 extra spectators attended his testimonial game than had frequented the regular home games.

BOSS OR FRIEND?

When ex-Latics players Keith Hicks and Vic Halom played together for Athletic they got along famously but when Hicks left Hereford United to team up with his old mate, who was then manager of Rochdale, he confessed that it was, "one of the biggest mistakes of my life", as he and big Vic just did not see eye to eye. Hicks picked up a bad pelvic injury in 1987 which cut short his playing career but he went on to become the director of Rochdale AFC's School of Excellence.

GIVE US A BREAK

Billy Johnston was signed from Glenavon in June 1966 and he was expected to become one of the key players in Jimmy McIlroy's team. In the first minute of the game on September 10th at Ayresome Park, Middlesbrough's Dickie Rooks tackled Billy with such a crunch that it put him out of action for the remainder of the season. The tackle was so severe that his right ankle was seriously fractured, requiring 30 stitches, and as a result the Latics were robbed of their inspirational midfielder. It was to be a cautious return when he stepped out for the reserves on March 18th in an attempted comeback. A complete recovery never came and he had to announce his retirement from the game in October 1968.

ROSE BOWL

The Rose Bowl challenge was a pre-season friendly fixture that was set up jointly by the *Rochdale Observer* and the *Oldham Chronicle* newspapers. It was once an annual event and used to be played, alternately, at Boundary Park and Spotland. As the teams moved apart in the league due to Athletic's success on the field, the game was not always played on a regular basis. In 1994, after an absence of six years, the game was revived at Rochdale. The previous meeting had resulted in a win for Athletic at Boundary Park but this event was a dour affair, not like some of the previous exciting encounters. The Spotland men won the game 2-1 and took back the bowl which had been held by Athletic for 13 years. The only highlight of the game was the Oldham goal, a 35-yard screamer from Latics defender Neil Pointon.

TRUST OLDHAM

For a long period of time in 2003, it appeared very likely that Oldham Athletic would cease to exist. In May 2003 TOASfT (The Oldham Athletic Supporters Foundation Trust) was formed by Alex Metcalfe and John Connelly to try to save the club from extinction and to also halt their slide from grace. They appointed directors and set about creating a source of income to aid the club's plight. In the June of 2003 they arranged a football match, the Millennium Allstars v Wembley Wizards, which saw Latics legends take to the Boundary Park pitch for the Trust's first fundraising event, which generated over £100,000. Their first meeting was held at Boundary Park in July and over 1,000 fans attended when the Trust was renamed Trust Oldham. In March 2004, the Trust invested £200,000 in Oldham Athletic Association Football Club 2004 and secured a 3% shareholding in the club, and a seat on the board. The Trust cice-chairman, Barry Owen was nominated as the first ever supporters' representative on the board of Oldham Athletic. Having a fan on the board of the club was vital in ensuring a debacle similar to that of the 'Chris Moore era' will never happen again unnoticed. Fundraising continued and in October the Trust purchased a minibus which was loaned to the club on an ongoing basis in a donation worth £20,000. In April, they contributed a further £20,000 towards the signing of Luke Beckett on loan from Sheffield United, which was followed up with a 'Latics Player Share' scheme aimed at assisting the club to sign players. The club's new owners, Danny Gazal, Simon Blitz and Simon Corney, have gone on record time and time again to underline what an important part the people of Oldham have played in saving their football club.

THE MOST IMPORTANT PENALTY

John Sheridan's history with the Latics goes back to May 11th 1991 and little did he know that he would be remembered for one act which would have a major bearing in the life of Oldham Athletic. Sheridan was the player who brought down Andy Barlow in the last game of the season to concede the penalty which Neil Redfearn converted. The kick allowed Athletic to win promotion to the First Division as champions after a break of 68 years.

PAY UP

Paul Moulden was signed from AFC Bournemouth in March 1990 for a then record fee of £225,000. The *Bournemouth Echo* declared in the following September that Athletic still owed the Cherries £169,000 from the deal. Under Football League regulations the buying club had to stump up 50% of the fee immediately with the balance being negotiated, but payable, within the following 12 months. Athletic had mutually agreed with the Cherries to pay off the remaining half of the fee at £9,375-a-month so in actual fact they only owed £46,875, and not the inflated figure as published in the newspaper.

PROGRESSIVE COACH INITIATIVES

Willie Donachie, who spent ten years as a player and assistant manager at Boundary Park, was a very progressive coach and liked to bring in new things that he had learned from watching other teams train after he came back from his visits around the world. He bit off more than he could chew with one particular initiative, however. Out of the blue, he tried to introduce the now accepted small, five versus five, possession game warm-up prior to a night game at Middlesbrough. The team quickly went three down so the next game the lads refused to do it – an insurgence, if you like, and the team promptly won. Willie protested strongly but on this occasion player power won.

COME IN NUMBER SEVEN

Neil Adams was a member of the famous Latics side that won promotion to the top flight and earned a Wembley cup final appearance, but he went through a spate of being substituted every game. It got to a stage where he could stand it no longer and it went to the extent that it finally made him take action. Before the electronic scoreboard, and electronic substitute board, was introduced to football the teams used large cardboard numbers to inform the fans and players who was being substituted. Neil raided the bag that they were kept in and lobbed the number seven board over the back of the stand prior to the game. Consequently, when the inevitable happened they could not find the number seven so he stayed on for the duration of the game!

YOU BUY HIM AND WE'LL KEEP HIM

When Liverpool paid a record fee of £250,000 to take 17-year-old Wayne Harrison to Anfield on January 9th 1985, manager Joe Royle arranged a clause to take him back on loan for the rest of the season in a deal which was unique at the time.

MIDWEEK LEAGUE WINNERS

Goals from Walker and Hill gave the Latics a 2-1 win at Southport in their first ever Lancashire Midweek League game on September 29th 1925. Athletic went on to win the league for the 1925/26 season. Their final results were: P14 W11 L2 D1 F36 A23 Pts 23.

FIRST COMMENTARY

One of the first ever radio commentaries was relayed to patients in both Oldham and Liverpool hospitals on April 29th 1954. Athletic took on Everton for the last league match of the season in which Athletic were already doomed to be relegated. Everton won the game 4-0 and thus got promoted to Division One.

BACKROOM STAFF

Stephen Wanless was appointed as the club physiotherapist in October 1981 but Ian Liversedge took over the role from July 16th 1984. Graeme Hollinshead was appointed as part-time youth development officer in September 1984 and at the same time Jim Cassell took the role of part-time scout to replace Colin McDonald.

JOBS FOR THE BOYS

In the 2005/06 season, after John Sheridan was appointed Athletic's manager, he promoted under-16s coach Tommy Wright as his second-in-command and also brought back Lee Duxbury to take charge of the reserve side. Youth boss Tony Philliskirk complemented the coaching staff which was now made up entirely of ex-Latics players.

JACK ROWLEY

Jack Rowley was appointed as Oldham Athletic manager in July 1960 to succeed Norman Dodgin under whose guidance the Latics had needed to apply for re-election to the Football League. Rowley had a good playing pedigree which began at the age of 17 when he signed professional forms for Wolverhampton Wanderers. When he moved to Bournemouth & Boscombe Athletic he promptly scored ten goals in his first 11 games and Manchester United came knocking and paid £3,000 for his services in 1937. He scored eight goals in one game when he guested for Wolves in the war that saw him selected to represent England against Wales in a wartime international. He held the United post-war scoring record with 30 goals in the 1951/52 season and the record remained until 1960. Rowley earned six England caps and netted four times in the match against Northern Ireland in 1949. He will be best remembered for the inspirational signing of Bobby Johnstone, the man whose era brought fans flocking to Boundary Park and resulted in Athletic winning promotion in 1962/63. Another achievement was the double signing of Bert Lister and Ken Branagan, an absolute bargain at £10,000 when they came from Manchester City. Other significant signings were Bob Rackley, Johnny Colquhoun, Jim Scott and the immaculate centre-half Alan Williams. Lister repaid Rowley's confidence with an amazing scoring record the culmination of which was his six goals he blasted past sorry Southport in the 11-0 record-breaking win on Boxing Day 1962. Athletic beat Hartlepools United by 6-1 on the final day of the season, a game that confirmed their promotion in front of 12,283 exuberant Latics fanatics, but Rowley's reward was that just three days later he was requested to resign from his managerial role due to what was described in the boardroom as 'internal dissention'. Rowley did return for a second spell in charge to take over from Jimmy McIlroy after he had resigned to undertake the coaching job at Stoke City. His second tenure ran from October 1968 to December 1969 but he could not turn around a struggling side. He was dismissed after a run of five consecutive defeats and an eight-game winless streak, including the embarrassment of losing at home to non-league South Shields in the FA Cup. Rowley also had managerial experience with Plymouth Argyle, Ajax, Bradford Park Avenue and Wrexham but he left the game to concentrate on running a newsagent's shop in Shaw. Jack died in Ashton-under-Lyne at the age of 79.

LATICS IN THE SOUTHERN LEAGUE

When Athletic first took out their lease at Boundary Park in the 1905/06 season they began lobbying the Football League to secure national recognition for entry into the league. With an estimated 28 votes needed by the member clubs one could imagine the disappointment when the final reckoning took place and only 17 votes had been cast in their favour. Their dream of league football was shattered. In desperation Athletic applied to join the Southern League with the reasoning that the senior status of the league would stand them in good stead for any future votes. However, their hopes were again dashed as they were pipped at the post by Bradford Park Avenue who had also applied for membership to the Southern League. The Latics were destined once again for another season in the Lancashire Combination.

OPEN DAY 1982

Over 2,000 visitors attended Athletic's third open day on August 22nd 1982. The weather was dismal with continuous rain but at around 1:30pm the sun came out, although it remained very windy. The events included a penalty competition against the Latics' Andy Goram, a water ducking stool and the Greater Manchester police dog display. Mossley band entertained the crowd but the blustery conditions put paid to the hot air balloon launch, which was expected to go ahead, but the attempt had to be aborted for safety reasons.

THANKS BERT

When Bert Lister scored his six goals in the 11-0 win against Southport on Boxing Day in 1962, he had to wait a long time – until 11 o'clock – for his thank-you from boss Jack Rowley. Bert recalled; "It hurt a little because he thanked the other scorers in the dressing room. It wasn't until later at a supporters' club dance, when they gave me a round of applause, that he said 'Well done'. We did not hit it off too well at the time, although we get on fine now. He used to get my back up, but I realise that it was done to get the best out of me. I would be dropped for an easy match and recalled when we were playing tough opposition. He knew I would go out to show him what I could do."

JOE ROYLE

Appointed Athletic manager on July 4th 1982, it took Royle until 18th March 1983 to make his first cash signing. He paid £21,000 to Bolton Wanderers to bring in midfielder Tony Henry. Also that year he signed Mark Ward for £9,500 from Northwich Victoria and also captured Martin Buchan, the ex-Manchester United defender. That summer witnessed the departure of John Ryan when Newcastle United paid a whopping £235,000 for him. On January 24th 1984, Royle sprung another coup when he paid Stockport County £52,000 to bring footballing nomad Micky Quinn to Boundary Park. It took time for his team to gel and they finished the 1983/84 season in a lowly 19th position. Athletic made history when Liverpool paid £250,000 to take 17-year-old Wayne Harrison to Anfield in a unique deal whereby they loaned the youngster back for the remainder of the season. Slight progress was made on the field with a 14th place finish for the 1984/85 season. Another big profit was made when Royle shrewdly sold Mark Ward to West Ham United in a £240,000 deal and his team finished a creditable eighth at the conclusion of 1985/86. Royle was rewarded with a three-year contract which he signed in May 1986. Always having an eye for a bargain, Joe pillaged Leeds United on May 21st and came away with Denis Irwin for free and Tommy Wright for £80,000. On the same day Darron McDonough joined Luton Town for a fee of £87,000 – a good day's business. In 1986/87 Athletic finished third with 75 points but they were cruelly knocked out of the first-ever play-offs by Leeds United. In October 1987 Andy Goram was sold to Hibernian for £325,000 but the following month Royle brought in Earl Barrett for a bargain £30,000 from Manchester City. More wheeling and dealing in March 1988 saw the arrival of Ian Marshall from Everton for £100,000 while Andy Linighan left to join Norwich City for £350,000. Athletic finished the 1987/88 season in ninth place with 65 points. Royle pulled off another masterstroke when he raided Manchester City again to capture Paul Warhurst for a bargain £10,000 in October 1988. Tommy Wright joined Leicester City at the end of the season for a £300,000 fee. On March 25th Royle paid out Athletic's record fee for striker Paul Moulden of Bournemouth for £225,000. The 1989/90 season was the well-documented 'Pinch Me' season *(qv)* and that summer saw the departure of Irwin to Manchester United in a £700,000 deal. The following year Royle built on his success, and with Richard Jobson coming in from Hull City for £460,000 and Mike Milligan leaving to Everton for £850,000, they finally clinched the championship to reach the First Division after an absence of 68 years. Milligan rejoined the Latics in July 1991 for £600,000 and Graeme Sharp also arrived from Everton for a fee of £500,000, along with defender Brian Kilcline from Coventry City at a cost of £400,000. To offset the costs Warhurst was released to Sheffield Wednesday for £750,000. In November 1991 Royle accepted the offer of a new three-year contract and in February 1992 he allowed Barrett to join Aston Villa for a club record fee of £1.7m, which still remains to this day. Athletic survived their first season by finishing 17th but they sold Kilcline to Newcastle United for £250,000. In May 1992 Royle went wild and made his record signing when he splashed £700,000 to bring in Ian Olney from Villa Park. In August Steve Redmond and Neil Pointon arrived from Manchester City while popular winger Rick Holden made the switch the other way. It was a nail-biting finish to the 1992/93 season as the Latics beat Southampton 4-3 on the last day to send Crystal Palace down. Marshall went to Ipswich Town in August 1993 for a fee of £750,000 and although the Latics played Manchester United in the semi-finals of the FA Cup they also lost their top flight spot on the last day of the season. The 1994/95 season started precariously and when Everton sacked Mike Walker on November 8th, Royle was appointed as their new boss. Royle always remained in close contact with Oldham and when John Sheridan was fired as Athletic boss in March 2009, a strange twist of fate brought big Joe back to his roots as temporary boss to see if he could try to rekindle the passion of the team. In his first stint Joe had been in charge for a total of 608 games and had taken the club to new heights with two FA Cup semi-finals, a League Cup final and promotion to the First Division. His return as interim manager was less spectacular as his team played nine games of which they lost four, drew four and won just one, and it came in Joe's last match in charge, an away fixture at Walsall on May 2nd 2009. The end of the match was an emotional moment for the fans as well as big Joe who may never manage again.

RECORD SHUT OUTS

Les Pogliacomi arrived at Boundary Park near the end of the 2001/2 season and in his first full campaign kept a club-record 19 clean sheets – which still stands today.

TRAINERS APPLY HERE

When Athletic were looking for a new first team trainer/coach in 1974, the shortlist included such famous names as Ray Kennedy, Kevin Bracewell and Eddie Hopkinson but Andy Lochhead was finally offered the job.

HIGH TO LOW

Athletic fans certainly have to experience a multitude of emotions while following their team. In the 1993/94 season, for instance, they managed to go from the dizzy heights of an FA Cup semi-final appearance at Wembley Stadium to the devastating low of being relegated from the top flight – all in the space of four weeks. After the euphoria of walking down Wembley Way to see their heroes almost put Manchester United out of the cup, things went from bad to worse. 'That' Mark Hughes goal really had a devastating effect on the club and they collected only two points from their last seven league games; hardly a recipe for success. They managed to throw away leads against Coventry City, Manchester City and Liverpool and the seven points that they wasted would have been enough to ensure their safety. With a backlog of fixtures, the Latics had to play four crucial games in the space of only eight days – simply too much to ask. Joe Royle's boys had done extremely well to complete three seasons at the highest level, but without the envious financial backing of other clubs, it was always going to be a struggle to remain there. Athletic were relegated at the end of the campaign.

AND BECKHAM FOLLOWED SUIT

Four of Athletic's players – Andy Lochhead, Ian Wood, Ian Robbins and Paul Edwards – were all granted permission to play in America during the 1974 close season.

LES POGLIACOMI: HOLDS THE RECORD NUMBER OF CLEAN SHEETS WITH 19

WHAT COMPETITION?

Some clubs in the country have a large pool of supporters to choose from but some are very isolated with many fans having to travel a fair distance to take in a league game. Oldham Athletic do not have such a luxury, as the Oldham public have no less than ten different teams in every division from the Premiership to League Two, and all within a travelling distance of approximately 25 miles. This does not even include the many local pubs that become the adopted homes of so many armchair supporters who prefer to sit in relative luxury to watch their 'heroes' from the city just ten miles down the road. These are the luxurious options afforded to the Oldham footballing public wishing to travel to a game from 'up town'. All distances are given from the Town Hall steps.

1.7 miles:	(L1)	Oldham Athletic Football Club	OL1 2PA
6.7 miles:	(PL)	Manchester City FC	M11 3FF
7.7 miles:	(L2)	Rochdale AFC	OL11 5DR
11.5 miles:	(PL)	Manchester United FC	M16 0RA
12.0 miles:	(L2)	Bury FC	BL9 9HR
12.4 miles:	(L1)	Stockport County FC	SK3 9DD
19.2 miles:	(L1)	Huddersfield Town AFC	HD1 6PE
20.6 miles:	(PL)	Burnley FC	BB10 4BX
23.8 miles:	(PL)	Bolton Wanderers FC	BL6 6JW
25.4 miles:	(PL)	Blackburn Rovers AFC	BB2 4JF

BIG GATE BUT NO GAME

More than 40,000 people crammed into Boundary Park on July 6th 1921, one of the best crowds seen at the venue. They were ex-servicemen, disabled soldiers, factory workers and schoolchildren who had gone to see HRH the Prince of Wales.

LONG CONTRACTS MEAN NOTHING

On March 1st 1973 Athletic appointed Tony Smyth as club secretary but he resigned just two days later due to ill health. The resignation made him the shortest-serving secretary in Football League history.

PLAY-OFFS 1986/87

Athletic have reached the dreaded play-offs on three separate occasions. The first time was in the inaugural season of the competition in the 1986/87 season. Under the old rules of three automatic promotion spots, the Latics would have walked away with the step up to the First Division as they finished the season in third spot, an amazing seven points clear of fourth-placed Leeds United. However, the Football League decided that the play-offs were a way of keeping teams interested in promotion and relegation right up to the end of the season. The first Second Division play-off game took place at Leeds United on 14th May 1987. In front of 29,472 fans, Athletic were on course for a commendable 0-0 draw. In the final minute, substitute Keith Edwards scored a vital goal to give Leeds the edge for the return leg that was to take place back at Boundary Park. Three days later Leeds crossed the Pennines for the return game and a nice goal from Gary Williams soon put the teams level. Ex-Leeds players Andy Linighan, Tommy Wright and Denis Irwin all played against their old club while Andy Ritchie, soon to be one of Athletic's most famous sons, played for Leeds. Minutes from the end of the match Mike Cecere headed what looked like the winner but United silenced the home fans when Edwards got his second last-minute goal in two games. The 2-1 final scoreline for the Latics, watched by 19,216 supporters, meant that Leeds went through on the away goals rule. It was a cruel way to miss out on promotion and many of the Boundary Park faithful were seen to be openly weeping at the end of the game.

CLUB RECORDS FOUND UNDER ROCHDALE ROAD STAND

In 1980 the Manpower Services Commission looked into the safety of Boundary Park. As a result, the terracing at the Rochdale Road end needed to be replaced along with the pitch perimeter wall. As standing capacity for 5,000 supporters was decided to be sufficient to cater for any occasion, the remainder of this section was provided with seating with provision for a number of executive boxes. During the inspection, many of the OAFC hand-written records were found under the stand in cardboard boxes. They had been open to all the elements and were irreplaceable. Had they been lost, many invaluable records of the club's history would have been gone for ever.

MATCH REPORTS

Long before the advent of the football reporter, it was left to directors and other club officials to record match events and many of them were quite scathing. Here's a compilation of some such recorded comments which were hand-written by Athletic's officials:

5th November 1921

In the Sunderland v Oldham game, a 5-1 defeat, a comment from C. Roberts declared; "A. Marshall, by carelessness lost the match ten minutes from time."

3rd September 1923

L. W. Adlam, who went on to make 290 appearances and score 10 goals in eight years at the club, was described as "rotten, no brains" in the game at Derby.

31st October 1925

Oldham drew with Chelsea 1-1. The referee was H. N. Mee from Mansfield and he was described as being, "very unfair: 1, allowed deliberate fouls by Chelsea to go unchecked; 2, refused to give penalties on three occasions – a) Chelsea player knocked down the Oldham player Ormston in the penalty area; b) Deliberately handled the ball in the penalty area. c) An Oldham player was receiving the ball in the penalty area when a Chelsea player deliberately pushed him yards away from the ball. To sum up the matter the referee appeared to have decided to allow Chelsea to win at all costs."

16th January 1926

From the *Daily Dispatch* written by Adjutant: "A Bolton correspondent writes to express his pleasure at my references to the clean football displayed in the cup tie at Oldham, together with the comment that it was what one had come to expect of our best teams in these days."

28th January 1928

"Athletic went to White Hart Lane for a fourth round FA cup tie at Tottenham Hotspur. Armitage was injured in the first 15 minutes and retired from the game. Grundy was also injured and left the field in the second half. Athletic lost 3-0 but under the circumstances all played with great pluck."

ONE MATCH WONDERS

Pop stars have 'one-hit wonders' but the Latics have 'one-match wonders'. The rare breed of footballers who have only actually made one appearance, or in some cases a substitute's role, for Athletic before moving on.

Joe Stafford	v Lincoln City (H)	12th Oct 1907
Matthew Brunton	v Blackpool (A)	1st Jan 1908
John West	v Leeds City (A)	23rd Apr 1909
Tom Pennington	v Burnley (A)	9th Oct 1909
Albert Franks	v West Bromwich Albion (H)	1st Mar 1913
Val Lawrence	v Derby County (A)	22nd Nov 1913
Hugh Lester	v Notts County (A)	23rd Jan 1915
Albert Chadderton	v Aston Villa (A)	20th Dec 1919
Alex Paterson	v Huddersfield Town (H)	7th May 1921
George Waddell	v Bolton Wanderers (H)	11th Sep 1922
James Glennie	v Wolverhampton Wanderers (A)	22nd Nov 1924
Roger Seddon	v Fulham (A)	23rd Jan 1926
John McCue	v Nottingham Forest (H)	1st May 1926
John Prince	v Leeds United (H)	10th Mar 1928
Clifford Foster	v Wolverhampton Wanderers (H)	6th Oct 1928
Harry Green	v Bristol City (A)	10th Nov 1928
Howard Baker	v Clapton Orient (A)	13th Apr 1929
Jack Hallom	v Bury (H)	16th Jan 1932
Llewellyn Purcell	v Bury (H)	16th Jan 1932
Harold Brown	v Chesterfield (H)	5th Mar 1932
Alan Milward	v Plymouth Argyle (A)	28th Mar 1932
Bill Baldwin	v Stoke City (H)	31st Jan 1933
Frank Britton	v Barnsley (A)	29th Sep 1934
Arthur Sharp	v Plymouth Argyle (A)	1st Dec 1934
Norman Alden	v Mansfield Town (A)	31st Aug 1935
Bill Ridding	v Chesterfield (A)	16th Nov 1935
Sidney Jones	v Wrexham (A)	30th Jan 1937
John Clarke	v Barrow (H)	17th Apr 1937
Jack Mayor	v Southport (H)	29th Mar 1938
Alwyn Fielden	v Rochdale (H)	31st Dec 1938
Bill Vallance	v Barrow (H)	28th Jan 1939
Norman Wood	v Southport (A)	4th Mar 1939

Tom Jones	v Carlisle United (A)	18th Mar 1939
Frank Eckersley	v Stockport County (H)	17th Apr 1939
Norman Wood	v Stockport County (H)	5th Oct 1946
John Divers	v Mansfield Town (H)	30th Aug 1947
Tom Dowker	v Rotherham United (A)	1st Sep 1947
Sam Walker	v Rotherham United (A)	1st Sep 1947
Norman Smith	v Hull City (A)	26th Aug 1948
Edmund Stringer	v Crewe Alexandra (A)	3rd Sep 1949
George Bradshaw	v Rotherham United (H)	19th Aug 1950
Harry Sharratt	v Derby County (A)	19th Mar 1956
Eddie Hartley	v Stockport County (A)	3rd Sep 1956
John Ferguson	v Scunthorpe United (A)	27th Apr 1957
Raymond Fox	v Carlisle United (H)	24th Aug 1957
Tommy Dryburgh	v Stockport County (A)	26th Aug 1957
George Sharp	v Rochdale (A)	14th Dec 1957
Kevin McCurley	v Northampton Town (H)	20th Aug 1960
George White	v Bradford Park Avenue (A)	27th Aug 1960
Barry Smith	v Gillingham (H)	3rd Sep 1960
John Horsburgh	v Bradford City (H)	9th Sep 1961
Peter Mitchell	v Southend United (A)	11th Mar 1966
Michael Faulkner	v Crewe Alexandra (A)	20th Sep 1969
Graham Schofield	v Wrexham (H)	1st Oct 1969
Jimmy Collins	v Fulham (A)	12th May 1984
Stephen Morgan	v Leeds United (H)	20th Oct 1987
Norman Kelly	v Stoke City (H)	9th Apr 1988
Chris Blundell	v Bournemouth (H)	7th May 1988
Winston Dubose	v Darlington (H)	11th Oct 1988
Simon Mooney	v Middlesbrough (A)	14th Dec 1988
Steve Bramwell	v West Bromwich Albion (A)	27th Mar 1989
Andy Gale	v Swindon Town (H)	13th May 1989
Orpheo Keizerweerd	v Liverpool (A)	10th Apr 1993
Mark Foran	v Tranmere (H)	4th Mar 1997
Alex Kyratzoglou	v Millwall (A)	11th Oct 1997
Danny Walsh	v Burnley (H)	10th Apr 1999
Neville Roach	v Millwall (A)	5th May 2001
Lee Hardy	v Port Vale (H)	21st Dec 2001
Rob Walker	v Brighton & Hove Albion (H)	9th Aug 2003
Rob Lee	v Hartlepool United (H)	30th Nov 2004

Amandou Sanokho..... v Sheffield Wednesday (H) .... 9th Apr 2005
Adam Legzdins .... v Chesterfield (H) .... 1st Nov 2006
Ben Turner.................... v Bournemouth (H) ....24th Feb 2007
Ashley Kelly .... v Leyton Orient (H) .... 12th Apr 2008

MAN OF THE MATCH WAS RUBBISH

On a pre-season tour of Sweden the players went out on an impromptu soiree the night before one of the games. During the match, the players who were not on the field had to listen to manager Joe Royle slaughtering David Currie's performance. The players did not agree with Royle's evaluation of his display as they thought that David had done well (given his condition earlier). When he was finally substituted by Joe he was immediately told that it was not good enough. Just then the announcement on the tannoy declared in pidgin English that the game's Man of the Match was none other than David Currie. David turned to Joe and said; "I am glad some f***er realises it." The comment was met with hysterical laughter all round.

HIGHEST AWAY GATES

The highest-ever league game attendance for Athletic was set at Old Trafford when they visited Manchester United for a Second Division game on March 31st 1975. A massive 56,613 turned up to watch the match. The Latics lost 3-2 but the goals from Ian Robins and Alan Young meant that Athletic were the first team to score two goals at the ground in that season. The largest First Division gate was set on September 27th 1913 when the crowd, which was estimated at 55,000, watched Manchester United bury the Latics by a score of 4-1. The FA Cup record was attained when Liverpool welcomed Athletic to Anfield on February 26th 1977, a 3-1 home win for Pool, which was seen by 52,455 spectators. The League Cup record was set on October 23rd 1996 when 36,314 crammed into Newcastle United's ground to watch the Magpies win a third round tie 1-0.

OLD-TIMER ROCKS LATICS

When Bryan Robson hit the mark against Athletic in the 1994 FA Cup semi-final replay he became Manchester United's oldest post-war goalscorer. He was 37 years and 92 days old.

TWO PLAYERS HIT ELEVEN GOALS

Newton-le-Willows visited Hudson Fold on January 7th 1905 in a Lancashire Combination 'B' Division game and returned home stinging from an 11-0 hammering. In one of the strangest ever goalscoring feats, centre-forward Plumpton scored the first five goals. Even stranger, the next six goals were all scored by inside-right Shoreman. Around 2,000 spectators watched the remarkable event.

THIRD DIVISION CHAMPIONS

Player-manager George Hardwick had set his sights high for the 1952/53 season and was going to accept nothing less than success. The campaign started with a remarkable 13-game unbeaten run that included a home and away double of 5-0 over Darlington Town. The first taste of defeat came in October with a 1-0 reverse at Gateshead, which was to be their only defeat in the first 18 fixtures. The run saw them sitting merrily on top of the league just one point better off than second-placed Grimsby Town. FA Cup wins over Boston United and Port Vale were followed by a 3-1 third round defeat at home to Birmingham City. The match was played in thick fog and the 26,580 supporters who had crammed into Boundary Park were lucky, or was it unlucky, to observe any of the goals. Loss of form after the turn of the year witnessed the league leaders winning only one game in 11 outings but their earlier season form meant that after their 1-0 home loss to Crewe Alexandra at the end of March, the Latics still topped the table with 46 points, albeit by goal difference. It left them just nine games to pull things back on course and they won four and drew four before travelling the short distance to Bradford City for the final game of the season. Many of the 23,580 fans had traversed the Pennines to see the event although the Oldham performance was well below par. Hardwick booted a goalworthy shot off the line and the Latics were reduced to booting the ball out of the ground to run down the clock. Centre-half Archie Whyte had a sterling game and confined Bradford to long range efforts as well as putting in some crunching tackles. Athletic could have sealed the win but their best chance fell to Bobby McIlvenny whose six-yard shot hit the Bradford keeper. However, a 0-0 draw was enough to give the Latics their first-ever championship in their history and it also gave the club the honour of becoming the first Lancashire club to ever gain promotion to the Second Division from the Third Division (North). The players were rewarded with a Wembley visit to witness the famous 'Matthews' cup final between Bolton Wanderers and Blackpool. The season ended with Athletic having an average attendance of 17,835, and left Eric Gemmell leading the scoring charts with 25 league and cup goals. The final league table was as follows:

Oldham Athletic	46	15	4	4	48	21	7	11	5	29	24	59	.7111
Port Vale	46	13	9	1	41	10	7	9	7	26	25	58	.9142
Wrexham	46	18	3	2	59	24	6	5	12	27	42	56	.3030
York City	46	14	5	4	35	16	6	8	9	25	29	53	.3333
Grimsby Town	46	15	5	3	47	19	6	5	12	28	40	52	.2711
Southport	46	16	4	3	42	18	4	7	12	21	42	51	.05
Bradford PA	46	10	8	5	37	23	9	4	10	38	38	50	.2295
Gateshead	46	13	6	4	51	24	4	9	10	25	36	49	.2666
Carlisle United	46	13	7	3	57	24	5	6	12	25	44	49	.2058
Crewe Alexandra	46	13	5	5	46	28	7	3	13	24	40	48	.0294
Stockport County	46	13	8	2	61	26	4	5	14	21	43	47	.1884
Chesterfield	46	13	6	4	40	23	5	5	13	25	40	47	.0317
Tranmere Rovers	46	16	4	3	45	16	5	1	17	20	47	47	.0317
Halifax Town	46	13	5	5	47	31	3	10	10	21	37	47	.0
Scunthorpe United	46	10	6	7	38	21	6	8	9	24	35	46	.1071
Bradford City	46	14	7	2	54	29	0	11	12	21	51	46	.9375
Hartlepool United	46	14	6	3	39	16	2	8	13	18	45	46	.9344
Mansfield Town	46	11	9	3	34	25	5	5	13	21	37	46	.8870
Barrow	46	15	6	2	48	20	1	6	16	18	51	44	.9295
Chester	46	10	7	6	39	27	1	8	14	25	58	37	.7529
Darlington	46	13	4	6	33	27	1	2	20	25	69	34	.6041
Rochdale	46	12	5	6	41	27	2	0	21	21	56	33	.7469
Workington	46	9	5	9	40	33	2	5	16	15	58	32	.6043
Accrington Stanley	46	7	9	7	25	29	1	2	20	14	60	27	.4382

LOST SHARES

J. W. Lees & Co (Brewers) purchased 18,000 shares from the executors of John Lowe (deceased) in June 1974 but the original share certificate was mislaid, or lost, and a new certificate had to be authorised.

BEST FA CUP WIN

Athletic recorded their biggest FA Cup victory on November 28th 1925 when West Lancashire League side Lytham visited Boundary Park. Played in atrocious conditions, the home side hit three goals in the first ten minutes in this first-round match. With a 6-1 half-time lead, a high score looked on the cards. Lytham's team contained six amateurs and fitness started to tell towards the end of the game. A crowd of 10,093 saw the Latics run out 10-1 winners. There was a minute's silence before the game in remembrance of Queen Alexandra who had died earlier in the week.

NEW SURROUNDINGS – NEW TACTICS

Athletic played their first game ever in their new surroundings of the Third Division (North) against Mansfield Town on August 31st 1935 and they went down 1-0. A club spokesman commented; "There is a greater dispersion in the Northern Section to make up for a lack of science with a little bit of 'extra vigour'. Well, we are down, and when you are in Rome, you must do as Rome does. We shall have to play them at their own game." Athletic finished the season in seventh place.

HAT-TRICK HEROES

The following players have notched up the following number of hat-tricks during their playing careers at Oldham Athletic: Eric Gemmell 8, Tommy Davis 5, Bert Lister 5, Roger Palmer 4, David Shaw 3, Bill Walsh 3, Harry Hancock 2, Frank Newton 2, George Taylor 2, Jack Pears 2, Ronald Ferrier 2, Fred Howe 2, Jimmy Frizzell 2, Colin Whittaker 2, Bob Ledger 2, Colin Garwood 2, Vic Halom 2, Rodger Wylde 2, Andy Ritchie 2, Stuart Barlow 2, Jimmy Faye 1, Alf Toward 1, Gilbert Kemp 1, Jim Marshall 1, Arthur Ormston 1, Horace Barnes 1, Albert Pynegar 1, Lawrie Cumming 1, Stewart Littlewood 1, Tommy Reid 1, Matt Gray 1, Ray Haddington 1, Peter McKennan 1, Alf Clarke 1, Kenny Chaytor 1, Tommy Walker 1, Dave Pearson 1, Gerry Duffy 1, Jim Mallon 1, Alan Shackleton 1, Steve Taylor 1, Micky Quinn 1, Mike Cecere 1, Rick Holden 1, Ian Marshall 1, Sean McCarthy 1, Scott Vernon 1, Chris Killen 1, Chris Porter 1, Luke Beckett 1, Lee Hughes 1 and Lewis Alessandra 1.

FRIENDLY GAMES 1921-76

The insignificance of friendly games means that the records of such matches always seem to be neglected. Here is a compilation of just a few of the friendly games that Athletic have taken part (or not taken part) in from the 1920s to the 1970s. On January 15th 1921 Athletic needed some goal practice. They played at Skelmersdale and drew 4-4 and then followed it up with a game at Rochdale on February 19th which resulted in a 5-5 draw. Sandy Campbell scored a hat-trick and Fred Broadbent and Tom Byron got the other goals. The Latics won 4-2 in a match at home to Northern Nomads on October 1st 1927 when Burgan, Wilson (2) and Fitton scored the goals. A benefit game for Moody's at Rochdale on May 2nd 1928 resulted in a 2-0 win in which Neil Harris and George Taylor got the goals and three years later, to the day, Jimmy Dyson and Fred Flavell scored the goals in a 2-2 friendly draw at Chesterfield. The reserves played a friendly fixture at Mossley on May 7th 1932 and fought to a 1-1 scoreline when Jack Roscoe got the reserves' goal. A game at New Mills was won by 3-2 on February 17th 1934. Another friendly success was achieved on April 26th 1934 when Prescot Cables were blown out 5-1. Norman Brunskil (2), Harry Rowley, Bill Hasson and George Pateman got the Oldham goals. On October 14th 1936 Athletic went to Northwich Victoria and returned with a 2-2 draw. Two Patricks, McCormick and Robbins, got the goals. In a match at Altrincham on January 22nd 1968, Reg Blore scored the only goal to give Athletic victory. Hunting Lambert Sports Services arranged a Latics v Internacional FC Brazil game on February 25th 1975 for a guarantee of £3,500. The game was subject to Football Association and Football League permission but never went ahead. On April 30th 1976 the Latics played at New Mills in aid of their new floodlights fund and goals from Maurice Whittle (2), Ian Robins (3) and Andy Lochhead gave the visitors a 6-2 win.

WHO'S GOT NERVES?

Andy Barlow does not appear to be the type of player who suffers from nerves before games. However, he confessed that he hardly ever slept a wink on Friday nights before a Saturday game.

"IF THEY'RE GOOD ENOUGH THEY'RE OLD ENOUGH"

Some young players at Oldham go on to make it big time while others are just a flash-in-the-pan. On May 12th 1945, manager Frank Womack gave a debut to 17-year-old centre-half J. B. Smith against Liverpool, but the youngster had a terrible time as the visitors won 7-0. Soon to be Bolton Wanderers and England hero Eddie Hopkinson made his debut for Athletic at Crewe Alexandra on January 12th 1952 at the age of 16 years and 75 days. He let in three goals in a 3-1 defeat but went on to achieve a remarkable 519 league and 59 FA Cup games in an 18-year career at Burnden Park. When Kenny Chaytor made his Latics debut on October 23rd 1954 at the age of 16 years and 11 months in a 2-2 draw at Gateshead, he became another of the youngest players ever to represent the club. Another young debutant, Stephen Morgan, stepped out as a substitute to make his only appearance on October 20th 1987 in the 1-1 draw with Leeds United at the tender age of 16 years 9 months and 22 days. Joe Makin played for Oldham in the 1967/68 season, at 16 years 7 months, and Matty Wolfenden was just 16 years and 115 days old when he first showed his studs in the 1-0 loss at home to Swindon Town on November 15th 2003.

COMMENTATORS' NIGHTMARE

In the 1931/32 season Oldham Athletic had three inside-forwards – Harry Johnson, Bill Johnstone and Billy Johnston – playing for them. Good job there weren't many commentaries around in those days!

MANAGER WANTED – WAIT A WILE

After the sudden departure of Jimmy Frizzell from Boundary Park, applications for the vacant manager's job in June 1982 included John Wile who was actually interviewed at Mr Stott's home. At the time he was playing for the Vancouver Whitecaps and the result of the interview was that he was offered the job for a period of three years, a deal which also included the transfer of Jimmy Frizzell's company vehicle. However, the job eventually went to a certain Joe Royle which led to a remarkable period in the history of the club.

ANOTHER RECORD ACHIEVED

Following the making of the Wembley record 'The Boys In Blue', with local TV and film stars Cannon and Ball, for the League Cup final of 1990, the players retreated to a pub in Oldham for a few drinks. They all needed some solace after all the stretching of their vocal chords but things got a little out of hand and the players overstayed their welcome. Prior to the quarter-final second replay at home to Everton in the FA Cup, manager Joe Royle requested Rick Holden's presence in his office and asked him for an explanation to which Rick denied all knowledge. Rick thought that he had kept his cool pretty well. At the beginning of extra time in the game (there is a famous photo of Royle grabbing Holden by his throat to back this up) it looks for all the world like he is saying, "Come on son, let's do it". In actual fact he said; "You had better win or else, because I know exactly what went on that Thursday afternoon and I know that you have lied." How did 'Sherlock' Royle know all this? All the players had signed the visitors' book on behalf of the landlord and he had invited Joe up to view the evidence!

GROBBELAAR BANKRUPT

Bruce Grobbelaar was one of the most entertaining and controversial goalkeepers around. The colourful character helped Liverpool to win the European Cup with his famous wobbly legged saves in the 1984 penalty shoot-out. In 1994 he was accused of match-fixing in conspiracy with a Malaysian betting syndicate but the courts cleared him in 1997. He later successfully sued *The Sun* newspaper for libel and was awarded £85,000. *The Sun* appealed against the decision and the judge reduced the award to £1 as there was "adequate evidence of dishonesty". With massive legal fees to find Grobbelaar was declared bankrupt. Latics manager Neil Warnock then signed Grobbelaar for Athletic on December 16th 1997 as goalkeeping cover. He was on non-contract terms and the 40-year-old made his debut towards the end of the 1997/98 season and he kept three clean sheets in four games, of which two were won, and two were drawn. He left Athletic to play for several non-league and lower placed Football League teams as well as coaching in South Africa and Zimbabwe.

PLAY-OFFS 2002/03

Over 12,000 supporters crammed in to Boundary Park on May 10th 2003 to witness Athletic's second ever venture into the play-offs. Iain Dowie had built a fine squad with a nucleus capable of holding their own in the First Division – so they entered the game full of confidence. Queens Park Rangers were the visitors and they too entered the game in aggressive form but their petulance in the match earned them six yellow cards and a sending off. David Eyres gave the Latics the lead in the 27th minute with a finely struck free kick that got deflected. Athletic's keeper David Miskelly made a blunder that allowed QPR a lifeline back into the game when his indecisiveness allowed Langley to force home an equaliser. The return match at Loftus Road just four days later was watched by over 17,000 passionate fans, including an estimated travelling army of Oldham fans of around 2,500. A large screen was set up at Boundary Park and the game was beamed back for approximately 4,000 supporters who couldn't get to Loftus Road. The game was a tense end-to-end struggle with the prospect of one flash of brilliance, or one mistake, which would probably be the only difference between the teams. Unfortunately, for the Oldham supporters, it was the latter. Another goalkeeping error, this time a bad long clearance from Les Pogliacomi in the 82nd minute, allowed the Rangers to win the match 1-0 and leave the Latics pondering a season that promised so much. The loss became the catalyst for Chris Moore to withdraw his funding from the Latics and send them into an uncertain future and possible extinction.

FIRSTS FOR YOUNGSTERS

In the match against Shrewsbury Town on December 18th 1971 it was a day of firsts for two of Athletic's youngsters. England youth winger Ian Buckley made his Football League debut and Ian Robins scored his first league goal. The feat was tarnished though as the Latics fell to a 4-1 defeat.

BRING YER BOOTS!

In the 1899/1900 season football was not quite as well organised as it is now and the Latics needed to beat Newton Heath Clarence to win the Manchester Alliance League. However, they showed up for the game with only seven players and lost 2-0.

MEET THE CHAIRMAN

Simon Blitz grew up in Hendon, London as a Chelsea supporter, which he still is to this day. He went to the USA in 1992 with very little money but with the hope of making his fortune. He started off selling cell phones, literally from a cart, and his business boomed into the huge telecommunications company Cellular Network Communications Group. He was a partner with Danny Gazal and they were joined by a further partner, Simon Corney, some four years later. The partners had always thought about buying a football club – any club – as the two Simons were admittedly football mad. When Oldham Athletic came on the market in 2003 the pair met in Toronto, Canada and they agreed to have a look at the homely little club which was commonly referred to as the Latics. Simon Corney went to Oldham on the following Tuesday and liked what he saw so the three agreed in principle to investigate the possibility of buying the club. Athletic was at the time in administration and the trio, affectionately christened 'The Three Amigos' (TTA) by the Latics faithful, realised that the club was in a run down state and would need considerable investment. Simon Blitz was appointed as chairman; Simon Corney became the managing director with Danny Gazal assuming the role of a director. The chairman regularly commutes back and forth from New York to attend to his footballing business. The purchase of the club opened the eyes of the new owners as it quickly became apparent that they would have to learn how to keep the lifeblood of the club, the supporters, happy. Oldham Athletic had a low base of fans and to compound the matter it was a low base of tough fans with extremely high expectations. The Three Amigos initially spent a considerable amount of money to keep the club in League One when, in hindsight, it may have been better if the team had been relegated so that they could have started again from scratch. The long-term plan for the future has never changed and TTA would like to build the club into one, with an adequate stadium, that could hold their own in the Championship. The chairman confessed that you can never do enough in the job and that it also takes over your life. If fans think it's a doddle they should step into the owner's shoes for a day and they would realise that it's not as easy as it seems.

ICE STATION ZEBRA

Athletic's Boundary Park ground was given the nickname of Ice Station Zebra due to it's relentlessly cold inhospitable climate, even in the summer months! Teams would never look forward to visiting Oldham especially on an icy cold winter's evening.

ALWAYS THE BRIDESMAID

Athletic are one of eleven teams who have reached the final of the League Cup but have never won it. The other teams are Rotherham United, Rochdale, West Ham United, Newcastle United, Everton, Southampton, Sunderland, Bolton Wanderers, Tranmere Rovers and Wigan Athletic.

FOUNDER MEMBERS

Oldham Athletic were founder members of the Premier League when it was formed in the 1992/93 season. Of the 22 clubs which contested that first campaign, there was only a total of 11 foreign players who strutted their stuff on the field. The Latics' representative was Gunnar Halle, the Norwegian international who won 24 of his 63 caps in his stay at Boundary Park. The other foreign players were Anders Limpar and John Jensen (Arsenal), Andrei Kanchelskis and Peter Schmeichel (Manchester United), Jan Stejskal (QPR), Roland Nilsson (Sheffield Wednesday), Michel Vonk (Manchester City), Eric Cantona (Leeds United), Hans Segers (Wimbledon) and Craig Forrest (Ipswich Town).

HEADS UP

When Roger Palmer was taking to the field for the second half of the game against Swindon Town on October 2nd 1990 he almost didn't make it. As he was heading down the steps from the tunnel he had his head bowed. Heading the other way, also with his head bowed, was the then commercial manager Alan Hardy. There was an almighty clash of heads! Roger was okay within minutes and he resumed play but Mr. Hardy was like a bear with a sore head for the next hour or so. Athletic won the game 3-2 leaving them still undefeated.

LIFE AFTER FOOTBALL

Ever wondered what's in store for the footballers who hang up their boots? Today's best players have it made with high wages, but years ago when the decision to retire and leave the game came along, many opted for taking coaching courses hoping to stay in the game either in a coaching role or in a managerial capacity. Here, alphabetically, are some of the more obscure occupations that some of the retired Latics players found themselves in after their footballing days were over.

Norrie Alden (1935-36): Worked for Bulmers Cider in Hereford.

Colin Barlow (1963): A successful businessman who in 1994 was part of a consortium that took over at Manchester City.

Earl Barrett (1987-91): Youth Sport Trust as a motivational speaker working with disaffected children.

Andy Barlow (1984-94): A regional coach for the Professional Footballers' Association.

Isaac Bassindale (1920-25): Draughtsman at Platt Brothers.

John Bazley (1956-61): Lecturer at Lincoln College of Technology.

Jim Beardall (1969): Ran his own printing business in Salford.

Ivan Beswick (1958-60): Became a successful businessman and retired to Guernsey.

Brian Birch (1959-60): A football coach who travelled the world to fulfil his appointments.

Bert Blackshaw (1936-38): Hospital physiotherapist in Wisbech.

Ronnie Blair (1966-69 & 1972-80): Director of a printing company.

Chris Blundell (1986-89): Worked at Hamilton Aerospace Corporation.

Jack Bowden (1938 & 1945-49): Was a qualified accountant who worked for Failsworth and Oldham Councils.

Bill Bradbury (1911-12 & 1919-20): Licensee in Burton-upon-Trent.

George Bradshaw (1950-51): Ran a newsagents and off-licence shop.

Tommy Broad (1909-11): Ran the Dudley Arms Hotel in Rhyl.

Fred Broadbent (1921-22): Entered the licensing trade.

Albert Broom (1924): Commercial traveller.

Martin Buchan (1983-84): Area manager for a large sportswear company then became a players' representative for the Professional Footballers' Association.

Johnny Burdess (1962-66): Joiner.

Peter Burke (1933-35): Bricklayer.

Kenny Chaytor (1954-60): Toolmaker.

Kenny Clements (1972 & 1979-85): Driving instructor and commissioned artist.

Tommy Davis (1935-38): Emigrated to Cannes.

Joseph Donnachie (1908-19): Took over The Mariner's Arms in Chester.

Harry Dowd (1970-74): Worked for John Willie Lees' brewery.

Winston Dubose (1988-92): Director of Business Development with Bayshore Technologies in Tampa Bay, Florida, USA.

Steve Edwards (1974-83): Company director at New Earth Water Services.

David Eyres (2000-06): Consultant for promising players outside the Premiership.

David Fairclough (1985-86): Partner in an independent investment company which advises players on the best way of taking care of their money. He also worked as a freelance journalist and in the insurance business.

Peter Floyd (1928-29): A miner at Calder and Huncoat Collieries.

Jimmy Fryatt (1970-71): Worked in Las Vegas casinos. Also worked as a mechanic, looking after the mowers and other machinery on a golf course.

Vincent Foweather (1920-22): Publican, ran the Savoy Billiard Hall and worked for Oldham Council.

John Gannon (1996-97): Ran his own soccer school in Sheffield.

Colin Garwood (1971-74): Worked for a transport company in Wisbech.

Wayne Gill (2001-03): Physiotherapist at Lancaster City FC.

Harry Grundy (1914-30): Auditor for the Players' Union.

Jimmy Hall (1963-67): Representative for a sportswear company who opened a sports shop in Bramhall.

Jon Hallworth (1989-97): Part-time goalkeeping coach at Boundary Park and also ran his own business in Stockport.

Vic Halom (1976-80): Worked for AMEC Utilities, a move from the football field to the computer field! He then became the Eastern European scout for Newcastle United.

John Hardie (1960-61): Self-employed joiner.

Jimmy Harris (1964-66): Steward at the Prenton Golf Club in Merseyside.

Wayne Harrison (1983-85): Ran a soccer School of Excellence in Blackpool and also worked as a drayman for Robinsons Brewery in Stockport.

Barry Hartle (1970-71): Postman in Stockport and also a taxi driver.

Bill Hayes (1936-51): Landlord of the Brighton Hotel in Oldham.

Tony Henry (1983-87): Players' agent.

Billy Hilton (1933-38): Taxi business owner, proprietor of the Windmill Garage in Royton, chairman of Royton Council and a Liberal councillor.

David Hodkinson (1961-64): Principal of a school in Ontario, Canada.

David Holt (1974-80): Owner of a plastics company in Haslingdon and also began a postal courier business in New Zealand.

Garry Hoolickin (1974-89): Licensee in Middleton and then worked in the property business.

Steve Hoolickin (1966-76): Worked in the building trade in Carlisle.

Leslie Horton (1944-47): Worked for Chloride in Manchester.

John Hudson (1982-86): Head of Community Liaison with the Professional Footballers' Association.

Jack Hurst (1947-51): Heywood publican before working in a pharmaceutical laboratory in Middlesex.

Billy Jeavons (1934): Engineer with Joseph Lucas.

Billy Johnston (1932-35): Licensee in Salford and Abergele.

Seth King (1929-32): Took the tenancy of the Castle Inn, Hillsborough and then ran a newsagent in Leigh.

Frank Large (1965-66): Owner of a bed and breakfast establishment in the Republic of Ireland.

John Liddell (1960-62): Lorry driver in Scotland.

Bert Lister (1960-65): Taxi driver in Blackpool.

Andy Lochhead (1973-79): Project director for New Earth Water Services.

Hugh McDonald (1910-11): Publican in Plumstead.

Mick McGuire (1985-87): Worked for the Professional Footballers' Association.

Ian McMahon (1980-84): Worked in the commercial departments of several rugby and football clubs before becoming the general manager of USA team Des Moines, Iowa.

Ted Malpass (1928): Joined the Wolverhampton Police Force and then worked as a physiotherapist on the Channel Islands. He also scouted for Nottingham Forest.

Ian Marshall (1988-93): Opened a restaurant in New Brunswick, Canada.

Jack Martin (1931-32): Coal merchant in Padiham and then a tackler in the weaving industry.

Stan Miller (1909-13): Yarn salesman for a Preston agency.

George Milligan (1935-38): Owned a holiday caravan site in Rhuddlan, North Wales.

Paul Moulden (1989-93): Ran a chip shop in Glossop.

Dick Mulvaney (1971-74): Worked in the dockyards in Sunderland.

Eddie Murphy (1956-59): Painter and decorator.

Martin Nuttall (1978-82): Financial advisor.

Ian Olney (1992-96): Partner in a Midlands fitted-kitchen company.

Eric Over (1957-58): Policeman at Grimsby Borough Police.

Elliott Pilkington (1910-26): Coal merchant in Radcliffe.

Sam Pilkington (1911-12): Cotton merchant who became the Mayor of Accrington and also president of the Lancashire Combination.

Beau Ratcliffe (1935-38): Family butcher in Birkenhead.

Matthew Rush (1997-98): PE teacher.

Fred Schofield (1933-36): Joined Oldham Police Force then became secretary of a local firm.

Joe Shadbolt (1905-09): Painter and decorator in Southport.

Tommy Shipman (1938-46): Licensee of the Willow Bank Hotel in Oldham.

Graeme Sharp (1991-97): Worked in media for the local press and radio in Liverpool.

David Shaw (1969-73 & 1975-78): Licensee of a pub in Newhey.

John Shufflebottom (1907-09): Agent in a timber merchant in the Birmingham district.

George Sievwright (1963-64): Manager with an electrical company.

Nick Sinclair (1978-84): Worked for the BBC in Manchester as a programme researcher and also worked for EDS, a computer services company in Stockport.

Bill Spurdle (1948-50 & 1957-63): Opened a tomato growing business in Guernsey.

Simon Stainrod (1979-80): Players' agent.

Jim Steel (1975-82): Joined the Merseyside Police.

Ernest Steele (1932-33): Groundsman at Barnsley and then at a public school in Tiverton.

Arthur Stenner (1957): Owned a furniture removal business.

Ron Swan (1964-67): Joined Oldham Police and used to patrol the pitch perimeter on matchdays.

George Talbot (1934-35): River policeman and worked in the north-east shipyards.

Barry Taylor (1963-64): Metallurgist.

Joe Taylor (1938): Licensee of the Nelson Inn, Union Street, Oldham.

Steve Taylor (1977-79): Gym manager in the prison service.

David Teece (1956-59): Draughtsman and fitter at British Aerospace.

Arthur Thompson (1969-70): Joined the Edinburgh City Police Force.

Ray Treacy (1975-76): Member of Professional Footballers' Association committee and ran a travel agency in Ireland.

Austin Trippier (1931-32): Stockbroker in Rochdale.

George Waddell (1922): Worked at Ribble Motors in Preston.

Tommy Walker (1954-57 & 1957-59): A Methodist lay preacher who also ran a newsagents shop in Middleton.

Charlie Wallace (1921-23): Painter and decorator in Birmingham.

Roy Warhurst (1960-61): Scrap metal dealer in Birmingham.

Albert Watson (1948-50): Opened a sports outfitters in Sunderland.

Alan Williams (1961-65): Worked as a caretaker in a complex of flats in Bristol. Also helped out by working behind his son's bar in Bristol.

Derek Williams (1956-59): Chartered accountant.

Gary Williams (1985-91): Ran a bar in Bristol.

Tommy Williamson (1935-46): Went into business in Fleetwood.

Ray Wilson (1969-70): Undertaker in Outlane, near Huddersfield.

Ian Wood (1965-80): Runs his own heating business.

George Woodger (1910-14): Fitter at Croydon Common Works Department.

Rodger Wylde (1980-83): He opened his own treatment centre/gymnasium near Sheffield and has been the physiotherapist at Stockport County for the last 20 years.

LEAGUE POSITION FINE BUT ATHLETIC FINED

Athletic forced a 0-0 draw at West Bromwich Albion on September 29th 1990 to retain top spot in the Second Division but they were fined by the Football League for showing up late for the match.

BRITAIN'S BRAINIEST FAN

Britain's brainiest football fan was officially crowned in 2004. The winner of the first ever Nationwide Football Mind Cup was Paul Prendergast, an Oldham Athletic fan. It was the inaugural year of the competition and Paul, now nicknamed 'The Professor' by friends, worked his way through to eliminate thousands of initial entrants before the competition was whittled down to a single super-brain. The national competition lasted nine months and featured seven rounds. The best scorer from each of the 92 English league clubs got to compete on the Nationwide Matchday Programme which was broadcasted across the country on the radio. Paul beat Premiership club counterparts as Arsenal came in at 48th, Chelsea a creditable 10th and Manchester United 39th overall! Blackburn propped up the entire table in 92nd place. Paul's runner-up was Kevin Mooney who was representing Crewe Alexandra, whom he beat 19-16 in a tense battle that went all the way to the final whistle. The then 27-year-old civil engineering estimator from Chadderton had been a fan of Athletic for 17 years after watching them beat Crystal Palace 1-0 in what was then Division Two in 1986. Paul commented: "Taking part in the Football Mind Final and being crowned as the Nationwide Football Mind champion was as thrilling for me as every time we manage to beat Manchester United or Manchester City – my favourite Oldham memories."

SCORING RECORDS: BIGGEST...

Cup Victory	13-1 v Parkfield Central, MJC	Jan 30th 1904
Victory (NL)	11-0 v Newton-le-Willows, LCB	Jan 7th 1905
Defeat (NL)	0-7 v Lower Crumpsall, MA	Feb 17th 1900
League Victory	8-3 v Nottingham Forest (home), D2	May 1st 1926
League Victory	11-0 v Southport (home), D4	Dec 26th 1962
League Defeat	9-0 v Hull City (away), D3(N)	Apr 5th 1958
League Defeat	4-13 v Tranmere Rovers (away), D3(N)	Dec 26th 1935

EIGHT MEN FINISH FA CUP GAME

On January 28th 1928, White Hart Lane was the venue for Athletic who took on Tottenham Hotspur in the FA Cup. Spurs won 3-0 in front of 36,826 supporters who paid receipts of £2,720 but the Latics were depleted with injuries and finished the game with only eight men on the field.

FIRST WEMBLEY VISIT

It was one of those fairytale endings to the 1989/90 season for Athletic as manager Joe Royle led his Second Division team out at Wembley on Sunday April 29th 1990 to take their place in the final of the League Cup. The match against Brian Clough's First Division Nottingham Forest was the culmination of a remarkable season in the history of Oldham. It all began back in September when Leeds United were beaten 2-1 in the second round first leg but when the Latics went to Elland Road for the second leg they surprised everybody with a similar result. Next up was a never-to-be-forgotten night for all that witnessed the Frankie Bunn show, an individual display where he bagged a record six goals in a 7-0 thrashing of Scarborough. In November, league champions Arsenal came to Boundary Park but went home with their tails firmly between their legs after two goals from Andy Ritchie and a stunner from Nick Henry easily put paid to the then current First Division leaders. Almost 15,000 people crammed into the ground to watch the home side progress to the fifth round, an away tie at First Division Southampton. Many fans made the long trip to the Dell but many were left disappointed as the ground was sold out and they couldn't get in to see the game. Matthew Le Tissier looked like he had won it for the Saints when he converted a penalty, his second goal on the night, with just five minutes of the game remaining. Ritchie had earlier scored a peach of a header to cancel out the first goal but he then stunned the home crowd when he poked home his 18th goal of the season late into injury time to earn his side a replay. Ritchie, who had scored in every round, and Mike Milligan were on target in front of another packed house of almost 19,000 at Boundary Park to give the Latics a comfortable 2-0 replay win which booked a deserved place in the semi-finals. More than 19,000 cup final hungry fans crushed into the ground for the first leg of the semi-final against another First Division giant in

West Ham United. Yet again, it was a case of how the mighty fall as Athletic's illustrious visitors returned home empty handed, this time to the tune of an amazing, and another record-breaking, 6-0 thrashing. No wonder the locals called the game the 'St. Valentines Day Massacre' after the 14th February tie! The second leg was a formality and although the Hammers regained some pride with a 3-0 victory, the Latics had their place firmly booked for their first ever visit to Wembley Stadium. Had Oldham Rugby won their own Challenge Cup semi-final, Wembley would have been inflicted with an enormous Oldham invasion as the rugby cup final was played the day before the League Cup game. In the final, Neil Adams almost put the Latics ahead in the opening minutes after he raced past England full-back Stuart Pearce and whipped over a deceptive cross which had Forest keeper Steve Sutton scrambling as it sailed just over the crossbar. Adams could have scored again soon after but his header was just wide. It was a sustained spell for the Latics minnows and Henry had a shot deflected for a corner before a rasping shot from Ritchie was tipped over the bar by Sutton. Forest countered and keeper Andy Rhodes had to be alert as he dived low to push aside a drive from Garry Parker in a half that was reasonably well controlled by Athletic although neither side could muster a goal. The game was settled by the only goal of the game when Nigel Clough put through Nigel Jemson who struck a shot which was initially saved by Rhodes, but Jemson was alert enough to follow up and put the ball calmly into the empty net in the 47th minute. Athletic did have their chances in the second half to take the game into extra time but it wasn't to be. Royle commented after; "One or two of the players showed the strains of the 61st game of the season. We have not been caught out on ability, but by a timetable which would have even stretched Liverpool. At the end of the day, we have been beaten at the highest level." The result did not spoil a great day out for around 30,000 Athletic supporters who made the trip south, some waiting decades, some flying in from abroad, to witness the game. It was still a memorable end to an unbelievable cup run. The final was later dubbed 'The Friendly Final' due to the good nature of the opposing fans. The Latics team was: Andy Rhodes; Denis Irwin; Andy Barlow; Nick Henry; Earl Barrett; Paul Warhurst; Neil Adams; Andy Ritchie; Frankie Bunn; Mike Milligan; Rick Holden. Bunn received a knee injury and was replaced by Roger Palmer after 67 minutes and Gary Williams was an unused substitute.

WHAT'S IN A NAME?

In December 2005, Latics fan Richard Metcalfe officially became 'Mr. Oldham Athletic'. The 24-year-old held such affection for his beloved club that he took the drastic step of changing his name by deed poll. The former Richard Andrew Metcalfe paid £34 to change his name to Richard Oldham Athletic Metcalfe. He said: "I came up with the idea of doing it for a bet. It's just one of those things, they jokingly put me up to it and I thought it would actually be a great thing to do, a way to permanently show my support for the club – although I do also have four Latics tattoos." Richard announced to his mum that he had a new identity. "She called me an idiot. I don't think she quite took it in at first but she's slowly coming around to the idea now. However, my original middle name, Andrew, was chosen by my godmother so it'll be interesting to see what her reaction is when she finds out!"

LEAGUE MAGAZINE DISCONTINUED

The club decided to discontinue using the Football League magazine for the 1974/75 season as the cost of £12 per thousand was prohibitive.

TWO-TIMING PLAYERS

There are a number of Oldham Athletic players who have enjoyed two or more playing spells on the books. Wartime guest appearances and returns as non-playing staff are not included:

Arthur Wildman	1904 & 1905-06
Don Travis	1951-52 & 1954-57
Bill Bottomley	1906 & 1907-08
Johnny Bollands	1953-56 & 1961-66
Paddy Stokes	1908-09 & 1910-11
Tommy Walker	1954-57 & 1957-59
Arthur Wolstenholme	1908-09 & 1919-20
Alan Ross	1956-57 & 1959
Bill Bradbury	1911-12 & 1919-20
Peter Stringfellow	1958-60 & 1964
Charlie Roberts	1913-15 & 1921-22
Johnny Colquhoun	1961-65 & 1968-70

Bill Goodwin .... 1913-21 & 1925-26
Ronnie Blair .... 1966-69 & 1972-80
'Sandy' Campbell .... 1920-22 & 1923-24
Les Chapman .... 1966-69 & 1974-79
James Naylor .... 1920-28 & 1933
David Shaw .... 1969-73 & 1975-78
Albert Broom .... 1921-23 & 1924-25
Kenny Clements .... 1972 & 1979-85
Harry Horrocks .... 1922-24 & 1926
Paul Atkinson .... 1977-83 & 1985-88
Frank Hargreaves ..... 1923-24 & 1925-30 & 1932-48
John Ryan .... 1978-83 & 1985-87
Arthur Ormston .... 1925-26 & 1928-30
Andy Goram .... 1981-87 & 2002
Tom Kellard .... 1926 (amateur) & 1926-28
Andy Gorton .... 1983-88 & 1991
Cliff Stanton .... 1927-29 & 1930-31
Mike Milligan .... 1984-90 & 1991-94
Alan Milward .... 1931-32 & 1936-37
Tommy Wright .... 1986-89 & 1997
Arthur Bailey .... 1933-37 & 1939-45
Ian Ormondroyd .... 1987-89 & 1996-97
Norman Wood .... 1937 & 1946
Andy Ritchie .... 1987-95 & 1997-2001
Jack Bowden .... 1938 & 1945-49
Rick Holden .... 1989-92 & 1993-95
Tommy Butler .... 1938-39 & 1946-47
John Eyre .... 1989-95 & 2001-05
Bill Waite .... 1942 & 1946-47
Neil Adams .... 1989-94 & 1999-2001
Ken Brierley .... 1945-48 & 1953-55
Mike Pollitt .... 1990-91 & 1997
Dennis Wright .... 1946-47 & 1951-52
Mark Allott .... 1995-2002 & 2007-09
Fred Ogden .... 1947-55 & 1956
Gareth Owen .... 2004 & 2005-06
Bill Spurdle .... 1948-50 & 1957-63
Ashley Kelly .... 2005-06 & 2007-08

RESERVE GAMES

Reserve games used to be an integral part of any avid football fan's week. Season ticket holders used to be admitted free of charge as part of the deal with their ticket purchase. Athletic's reserves were not in a recognised league in 2008/09 but arranged selected friendly matches and played in cup competitions. In a Central League game played at Stalybridge on September 6th 1919, goals from Gee and Lord gave Athletic a 2-2 draw in a match that contained an Oldham team with six amateurs in the side. Gates in the olden days were certainly much better that they are today. As an example, in the 1920/21 season, the Central League reserve matches brought supporters that many of today's current senior teams would envy. The lowest reserves gate was recorded as 2,149 with the highest being a staggering 8,626. Admission to watch the games was 8d for adults and 3d for children. Athletic used 31 players that season. For the 1982/83 season, the club were accepted to play in the new Lancashire FA senior cup. Burnley (A) on August 14th, Bury (H) on August 17th and Rochdale (H) on August 21st were the opposition. The club also applied to join the Central League where the midweek games were played in two divisions of sixteen clubs. Due to cost cutting it was suggested in March 1982 that the B team should resign from the Second Division of the Lancashire League. As a £1,000 fine would have been imposed, it was decided to complete the season then review it later. Athletic are again fielding a reserve side.

'F'OWL – YOU'RE OFF!

Did you hear the one about the Latics' mascot 'Chaddy The Owl' being sent off? It happened at Boundary Park on 26th August 2001 during the league match against Peterborough United. The linesman 'flagged' Carlo Corazzin for offside. As there were three defenders between Carlo and the goal this seemed like a poor decision, one that is not unusual at Boundary Park. After consulting with the referee it was found that the linesman had mistaken 'Chaddy' for Carlo and gave the owl offside. After much discussion on the touchline, Chaddy was shown a red card and had to go off. The game was lost 4-1 and the supporters claimed that we never got over losing Chaddy so early on in the game.

THE BIG TIME AT LAST

Newcastle United, FA Cup holders and a First Division powerhouse, provided the opposition for Athletic's first-ever home game in Division One on September 10th 1910. A record of 34,000 excited fans crammed into Boundary Park to witness the event on a glorious day brimming with sunshine. The gate remained unbeaten until 1930. Unfortunately, for the Latics fans, Newcastle won the game 2-0.

NON-FOOTBALL ACTIVITIES AT BOUNDARY PARK

Boundary Park has been used for many events over the years. A parachute display was granted for October 19th 1975 and a brass band contest took place on June 5th 1976. The TV competition, run by Don Robinson (Holdings Limited) of Scarborough, *It's A Knockout*, was staged on the ground on May 19th 1977 and in July 1979 The Watch Tower Bible and Tract Society paid the Latics a sum of £3,500 to hold two assemblies, although the assemblies needed the permission of the Football League. At the Bristol Rovers game on February 7th 1981, the half-time entertainment on the pitch was a display of martial arts.

AUSTRIA AND HUNGARY TOUR

In today's game pre-season tours are the norm, but Athletic were ground-breakers in this area as they took part in a tour of Austria and Hungary at the beginning of the 1910/1911 season. The Latics had just gained promotion to the First Division for the first time and they were invited on the 12-day tour. The tour was contested by Athletic, Blackburn Rovers, Vienna Association, Budapest Athletic, Magyar Testgyakoriok and Ferencvarosi Torna. Little is known about the tour but Tommy Broad played against Wiener Sporting Club in Vienna, the club which donated and presented a silver cup for the winners. The silver cup was valued at £20 and Oldham and Blackburn contested the final which was over two legs. The first leg was played on May 28th 1911 and Athletic won 1-0, but the second leg on May 31st 1911 was a blow-out with Rovers convincing winners by 5-2. It is assumed that the cup still resides in the Ewood Park trophy room but this is unconfirmed by Blackburn.

HURST REWARDED FOR HIS APPEARANCES

A presentation was made to John Hurst at the Bristol Rovers game on February 7th 1981 to recognise the fact that he had completed a total of 500 Football League appearances.

TWINS LINE UP TOGETHER

On May 4th 1997, twins David and Scott McNiven played in the 3-0 win over Norwich City. Goals from Matty Rush and Stuart Barlow and an own goal by ex-Latic Neil Moore gave Oldham the victory. It was a good end to a bad season as Athletic were relegated along with Grimsby Town and Southend United. When David came from the bench in the 80th minute of the game, it was the first time that twins had ever played in the same Oldham Athletic team. The Latics' other twins Paul and Ron Futcher had both played for Athletic in the 1980s, but had never appeared in the same team together.

LEADING GOALSCORERS

Since Athletic were formed as Pine Villa, and as scant records have been kept of the earliest games, it has been difficult to establish credible goalscoring results. Some of the earlier games recorded did not include Christian names and many of the players and goalscorers will forever remain unknown. The following records of such pioneering marksmen are deemed to be correct from the information available. They include all matches – league, cups and friendlies:

Pre-Football League

Manchester Alliance............... 1899/00 ....Joe Sankey............. 19 goals
Lancashire Combination 'A' .. 1906/07 ....Joe Shadbolt.......... 32 goals

Football League

Second Division...................... 1907/08 ....Frank Newton....... 30 goals
Third Division (North).......... 1935/36 ....Billy Walsh............ 37 goals
Third Division (North).......... 1936/37 ....Tommy Davis .... 38 goals

OLDHAM ATHLETIC SUPPORTERS' CLUB

The official Oldham Athletic Supporters' Club was formed back in 1924. Five locals – Edwin Henthorn, Tom Farrow, Alf Haig, Arthur Beadsworth and Willy Hudson – met at number 7 Glodwick and established the club. The gang of five decided to raise funds for the club that was a daunting task as trade in those days was bad. They were joined the following year by Vincent Winterbottom who remarkably remained with the supporters' club until he retired as chairman in 1965. During his many years of service he held almost every office available. The supporters systematically worked their way around the ground and did up all the terracing. Fundraising ideas were hard to come by but they raised cashed with the following schemes: Latics scent cards; Latics pencils; Penny on the Ball; garden parties; jazz band contests; boxing; and stop-watch competitions. The motto of the club is "Help not Hinder".

OFF TO A FLIER

A 1-0 loss at Port Vale on November 17th 1990 ended Athletic's remarkable record-breaking start to any season. Oldham had gone 16 league games without defeat but the loss still left them sitting pretty at the top of the Second Division league table.

STAR FINDER

Colin McDonald was the Latics' chief scout back in the 1980s. One of the best goalkeepers around, he had played 201 games for Burnley but he broke his leg on March 17th 1959 when playing for the Football League in an inter-league game in Dublin. The injury cut short a promising career and the respected McDonald could have gone on to break all the England international appearance records if not for the injury. Previously a scout at Bury, he found talents like Colin Bell, Eddie Colquhoun, Jimmy Kerr, Alec Lindsay and Terry McDermott who all went on to represent their countries at various levels. He moved to Bolton Wanderers and in a ten-month spell unearthed the likes of Neil Whatmore, Paul Jones and Barry Siddall. McDonald continued the trend at Athletic and his earlier finds included the likes of Gary Hoolickin, John Humphries, Paul Heaton, Paul Atkinson, Nick Sinclair, John Ryan and Darren McDonough.

WOLSTENHOLME CLOCKS UP 25 YEARS

In today's crazy world of revolving door coaches, Athletic's Frank Wolstenholme deserves a special mention. Frank has just completed 25 years as a coach at the Latics' Centre of Excellence. He has remarkably served under nine different managers and has gone through massive changes in the way that young players at football clubs are nurtured. Frank is a health and welfare manager with Manchester City Council but spends two evenings every week working with the under-12s and then he takes them for matches on Sunday mornings. He told the *Oldham Chronicle*, "It is hard to believe I have been at the Centre of Excellence for so long as the time has flown by. I can honestly say I have enjoyed every second and gained a lot of satisfaction helping youngsters to improve their games." He had spells as a player with Blackburn Rovers and Stockport County but his playing career was mainly in non-league with local teams Ashton United, Droylsden, Curzon Ashton and Glossop. Frank went on; "It was the days of the plastic pitch and we would train on that. Bill Urmson would work with the 15-16 year-olds and Willie Donachie and Graeme Hollinshead the younger lads. The coaches changed in the referee's room at Boundary Park and I would be sat there when the likes of Colin Bell and Rodney Marsh, star players in my eyes, would turn up. It was great for the lads and on one occasion they couldn't get the ball off Rodney. It is little things like that which stick in my mind." Frank has worked with England under-21 player Paul Gerrard, who later had a big-money move to Everton, Lee Darnborough and Andrew Woods, who both became England schoolboy internationals, and Paul Bernard, Paul Rickers and Richard Graham who all went on to establish themselves as first team regulars at Boundary Park. Daniel Philliskirk and Aaron Chalmers were also coached as under-10s and became trainees. Philliskirk later landed a dream move to Chelsea. Philliskirk's dad Tony, who also starred as a player for Athletic, has helped Frank to bring an air of professionalism to the Centre of Excellence. Frank has rated Joe Royle, Iain Dowie, Andy Ritchie and John Sheridan as his favourite managers to work under.

HIGH SCORER

Tommy Davis racked up a total of 39 goals in the 1936/37 season. They comprised of 33 league; 2 FA Cup, 3 NS Cup and one Lancashire Cup goal.

MR CONSISTENCY

Ian Wood played a record 585 games for Oldham between 1965 and 1980. He made his debut as an 18-year-old in the 2-0 home loss to Queens Park Rangers on May 25th 1966 and had also clocked up 26 goals by the time he left Boundary Park. Wood was first spotted playing in the Sunday League in nearby Radcliffe and was signed by Gordon Hurst as an amateur. Initially, he began his career as a centre-forward and when Jimmy McIlroy took over at the helm his squad was boosted by the big money spending of new chairman Ken Bates, and Wood was left to spend his time waiting for his opportunity and playing in the reserve side. He took his chance when Frank Large left Athletic for Northampton in the 1966/67 season. The campaign started with only one win in the first twelve matches but then the Latics then went on a run of seven straight victories in which Wood played an integral part, albeit as a utility player, as he appeared in all three inside-forward positions; both full-backs and at wing-half. He settled down into the right-back position after Jimmy Frizzell took over as manager and thus began a remarkable run of consecutive games. Wood was injured when he dislocated his shoulder on April 27th 1974 after he fell badly in the game at York City and he was unable to play in the next fixture. It concluded an unbroken run of 161 matches that went back to 1970. The popular blond-haired defender broke the previous all-time appearance record for the Latics when he came on as substitute against West Ham United on April 29th 1980. The record had been held by David Wilson who had amassed a remarkable 263 games. Wood had a spell in America with Denver Dynamos and later joined Burnley. He was awarded loyalty bonuses in November 1973 and April 1974 for a period of two years. His son Clark also signed for Athletic as a trainee but failed to make the senior level. Wood ended his playing career back at his home town at Radcliffe Borough and eventually ended up as chairman of the club.

BABY LATICS

A new Latics fan was born in January 2009. Little Joshua Kindon appeared into the world and his parents Andrew and Gaynor decided to give their son the middle name 'Latics' in honour of the club.

SIGN HERE PLEASE

The weirdest autograph that former Latics striker Rodger Wylde ever signed occurred when a male fan asked him to sign on his backside. Wylde duly obliged but was probably grateful that the fan didn't want kisses on the bottom!

FRIENDLY GAMES 1981-DATE

Here are some of the friendly games that Athletic have taken part in from the 1980s up to the present date: A 1982/83 pre-season friendly on August 10th was won 2-0 at Macclesfield when Paul Heaton and Steve Edwards got the goals but Athletic lost 2-0 at home to Everton on August 19th 1983. For the 1984/85 season the first visitors were Stoke City on August 15th and the Latics won 3-2 with goals from Derrick Parker (2) and Mark Ward. A 0-0 draw at Rochdale on August 8th was followed by a trip to West Bromwich Albion on August 18th which resulted in a 1-0 loss. The fixture at Macclesfield was played on August 11th 1984 and Athletic again went down 1-0. When Oldham welcomed Manchester United to Boundary Park on January 20th 1985 they lost the game 2-1 and teenage star Wayne Harrison scored for the home side. Gary Hoolickin's testimonial game was a friendly against Manchester City on September 9th 1986. It was a hard fought game with a 3-3 scoreline. Paul Atkinson, Tony Ellis and Ron Futcher notched for Athletic. The Latics lost by 1-0 at home to Hibernian on August 6th 1988. Wrexham welcomed Athletic to the Racecourse on August 18th 1990 where goals from Andy Holden and Neil Redfearn gave the Latics a 2-1 win. Roger Palmer's testimonial was played at Boundary Park on May 14th 1991. Manchester City were the visitors and Palmer scored the second goal in a 3-2 win in front of 15,700 fans. Port Vale entertained the Latics on August 10th 1991 and beat them 2-1 with Rick Holden notching Oldham's goal. Everton visited Boundary Park for Frankie Bunn's testimonial game on August 9th 1994. Goals from Holden and Sean McCarthy gave the Blues a 2-2 draw. In a match on July 30th 2008 John Sheridan's brother Darren, who manages Barrow, invited Oldham for a friendly game at Holker Street. Barrow won 3-1 in front of 480 supporters. Bradford City played Athletic and beat them 1-0 on a hot, sweltering August 2nd 2008.

SCOTLAND INTERNATIONALS

The following Latics players have represented Scotland at international level but not necessarily while they were playing on Oldham's books. All levels of representation are listed in chronological order:

Finlay Speedie	1908-09	3 caps and 1 SL Xl app
Joseph Donnachie	1908-19	3 caps
David Wilson	1906-21	1 cap
John McTavish	1910	1 cap and 2 SL Xl apps
Alex Paterson	1921-22	junior
Neil Harris	1927-29	1 cap
Billy Johnston	1932-35	junior
John Divers	1947	1 cap
Peter McKennan	1951-54	2 SL Xl apps
Tommy Wright	1957	3 caps
Bobby Johnstone	1960-65	17 caps, six SL Xl apps and one GB app
Arthur Thompson	1970-71	schoolboy and U-23
Tommy Bryceland	1970-72	schoolboy and U-23
Colin Garwood	1971-74	youth
Bobby Collins	1972-74	31 caps and 15 SL Xl apps
Andy Lochhead	1973-79	U-23
Steve Gardner	1977-81	schoolboy
Alan Young	1974-79	schoolboy
Andy Goram	1981-87	25 caps
Martin Buchan	1983-84	youth, U-23 and 34 caps
Joe McBride	1983-86	schoolboy and U-23
Willie Donachie	1984-93	U-23 and 35 caps
Gordon Smith	1986	U-21, U-23 and 1 cap
Tommy Wright	1986-89 & 1997	youth and U-21
Asa Hartford	1989	50 caps
Scott McGarvey	1989-90	U-21
Paul Bernard	1990-94	U-21
Graeme Sharp	1991-94	12 caps
Craig Fleming	1991-96	U-21
Mark Innes	1994-2001	youth
Scott McNiven	1994-2002	U-21
Gerry Creaney	1996	U-21 and 'B' level

John McGinlay..........1998-99..'B'level and 13 caps
Andy Liddell..............2005-09...U-21
Gary McDonald........2006-08..............................U-16 to U-20 and 'B'level

YOU'VE NEVER BEAT THE LATICS

Oldham Athletic have crossed swords with many teams in their long history and some teams have never beaten the Latics. Taking league games and FA Cup games into consideration, the following teams have yet to taste victory against Athletic:

Boston United	P1	W1	L0	D0	F2	A1
Burton Albion	P2	W1	L0	D1	F4	A4
Chasetown	P2	W1	L0	D1	F5	A1
Crook Town	P1	W1	L0	D0	F1	A0
Croydon Common	P1	W1	L0	D0	F3	A0
Denaby United	P1	W1	L0	D0	F2	A0
Ferryhill Athletic	P1	W1	L0	D0	F6	A1
Formby	P1	W1	L0	D0	F2	A0
Gainsborough Trinity	P6	W5	L0	D1	F15	A3
Grantham Town	P2	W2	L0	D0	F7	A1
Hednesford Town	P1	W1	L0	D0	F4	A2
Kettering Town	P1	W1	L0	D0	F4	A3
Kidderminster Harriers	P1	W1	L0	D0	F5	A0
King's Lynn	P1	W1	L0	D0	F2	A0
Lancaster City	P1	W1	L0	D0	F6	A0
Northwich Victoria	P1	W1	L0	D0	F3	A1
Rhyl	P1	W1	L0	D0	F1	A0
Shildon	P3	W2	L0	D1	F9	A3
Thornaby-on-Tees	P2	W2	L0	D0	F10	A4
Thurrock	P1	W1	L0	D0	F1	A0
Walthamstow Avenue	P2	W1	L0	D1	F5	A3

The victory over Burton Albion was achieved after a penalty shoot out, which the Latics won 5-4. In addition to the above results, Glossop North End, Leeds City, Nelson, New Brighton, Newport County, Oxford United, Rushden & Diamonds and Scarborough have never won on a visit to Boundary Park.

ADMINISTRATION

The club were forced into administration during the October of 2003 and things started to look extremely bleak for the club as the financial crisis worsened and no saviour could be found. Peter Ridsdale, having left Leeds United in debt, threw his hat into the ring as a potential 'knight in shining armour' but he did not endear himself to Latics fans after claiming that the club was beyond being saved. A short period after this set-back several suitors evolved, one a Norwegian consortium led by one Vidar Fossdal who came very close to 'buying' the club. Despair set in when it came to light on the eleventh hour that the group were in fact cruel hoaxers who had no real financial backing. The club had literally only hours to live when an American consortium, who had previously looked at Hull City and Huddersfield Town, expressed an interest in the club. They agreed with the administrators to fund the £250,000 monthly deficit and with due diligence they took control of the club. Several months later they were announced as Danny Gazal, Simon Blitz and Simon Corney – aka the 'Three Amigos' – and they took ownership of the club as well as purchasing Boundary Park and the surrounding land. The Three Amigos sold 3% of the club for £200,000 to Trust Oldham, the supporters' trust. In return for the investment, the Trust would hold an unconditional seat on the board of directors, the first time a supporter had ever been given this privilege in the history of the club.

HE'S A KEEPER

In the 2006/07 season the club used no less than seven goalkeepers at first team level. The keepers used were; Les Pogliacomi, Chris Howarth, Terry Smith, Ryan Smith, David Knight, Adam Legzdins and Alan Blaney.

HATE MAN UNITED?

Latics record appearances star Ian Wood has admitted that he is a Manchester United fan, and to make things worse he is also a former season ticket holder at Old Trafford. He has eventually seen the light though and no longer watches any football matches, with the exception of his grandchildren's games. Ian said that the best player he has ever faced is Alan Groves, another former Latic.

RHODESIA AND MALAWI TOUR – 1967

The tour was shrouded in controversy and a Mr. Faulds asked the Secretary of State for Commonwealth Affairs if Her Majesty's Government were aware of the visit of Oldham Athletic football team to Southern Rhodesia; and why he was allowing this tour. Mr. George Thomas stated that Her Majesty's Government were aware of this visit and he commented; "We deplore organised tours of this kind while the state of illegality exists in Rhodesia, and we made our views clear to the Oldham Athletic Football Club before the team left. We have no powers, however, to prevent private citizens from going to Rhodesia." The British Government tried to get the exclusion of Rhodesia from the 1968 Mexico Olympics but their inability to exert any control over British sporting organisations proved to be a cause of embarrassment in its efforts to gain international support for Rhodesia's exclusion from the Games. Despite its efforts to persuade other nations to isolate Rhodesia from international sport, it was unable itself to prevent British sporting bodies from maintaining contacts with Rhodesia. Although the government had been able to persuade some organisations from visiting the Republic, most notably, the Yorkshire County Cricket Club, a number of tours did go ahead. The full tour was as follows:

June 18th........v St Pauls (Rhodesian Champions) in Salisbury............6-0
June 21st.........v Rio Tinto in Que Que..2-3
June 24th........v FAR Xl (FA of Rhodesia) in Bulawayo 3-1
June 25th........v Dynamos (National League North) in Salisbury........4-2
June 28th........v Mangula FC in Mangula 4-0
July 1st............v Great Dykes Association Xl in Mtorshanga................7-3
July 1st............v Tornados in Salisbury...3-2
July 2nd..........v Manicaland Xl in Umtali..2-1
July 4th...........v Salisbury Callies in Salisbury..5-2
July 6th...........v Malawi FC in Blantyre...6-2
July 8th...........v Blantyre Sports Club in Blantyre....................................6-2

BEHIND ME

Neil Adams, signed from Everton for £100,000, was a member of the team promoted to the top flight. He always used to insist that he was one of the first four players when the team lined up to enter the field of play.

THERE'S ONLY TWO...

The following Latics players have shared the same name:

Paul Francis Edwards 1972÷77 & Paul Anthony Edwards 2005-07
Craig Fleming 1991-97 & Craig Mathew Fleming 1997-2004
John Hurst 1947-51 & John W Hurst 1967-81
William C. Johnston 1966-68 & William Gifford Johnston 1932-35
George Alexander Jones 1973-76 & George Benjamin Jones 1932
Paul Bernard Jones 1985-87 & Paul Neil Jones 1999-2002
Thomas Jones 1919-20 & Thomas Jones 1939-40
John William McCue 1925-26 & John William McCue 1960-62
Robert Scott 1959-60 & Robert Scott 2005-06
George Shaw 1908-10 & George David Shaw 1969-73
George Taylor 1923-29 & George Barry Taylor 1963-64
Joseph Taylor 1929-31 & Joseph Thomas Taylor 1938-46
James Thompson 1920 & James Thompson 1952-58
Thomas Wright 1957 & Thomas Elliott Wright 1986-1989, 1997

BOOT IT – RIGHT?

When Bert Lister scored six goals in the 11-0 humbling of Southport on Boxing Day in 1962, the result equalled their highest ever score but beat their highest ever league victory. An amazing fact was that all six of Bert's goals were scored with his right boot!

THE JONES BOYS

Over the years Oldham Athletic had enough players named Jones to provide a full team and substitutes. Here is the team: Alex Jones, Arthur Jones, Charles Jones, Chris Jones, Ellis Jones, Evan Jones, George A. Jones, George B. Jones, John Jones, Paul B. Jones, Paul N. Jones. Substitutes: Richard Jones, Sidney Jones, Tom Jones, Tom Jones, Daniel Jones.

EARLY GOAL

Middlesbrough scored a first minute goal in the First Division match at home on October 18th 1919, a game which resulted in a 2-1 loss for the Latics.

SAN-AN CUP 2005

At the club's directors' meeting on April 8th 1982, a tour of Ibiza was arranged which was provisionally arranged to commence on June 5th 1982. It was agreed that the tour should go ahead on the condition that Ibiza, Valencia and possibly Borussia Monchengladbach would form some of the opposition. Athletic's build up for the 2005/06 season, also in Ibiza, was arranged by Holiday Experience and the players agreed to provide their own spending money. The San-An Cup was played between the dates of 2nd and 9th July and the club took the following squad: Pogliacomi, Murphy, Forbes, Griffin, Lever, Owen, Scott, Stam, Tierney, Bonner, Edwards, Hughes, Warne, Wellens, Butcher, Todd, Eyres, Facey, Killen, Liddle, Porter, Hall. The Blues kicked off their pre-season tournament in fine style with a convincing 7-0 hammering of UE San Jose, Ibiza's local team, on July 6th. Andy Todd was an Athletic trialist and he scored a hat-trick on his club debut against the Spanish part-time team. Chris Killen also bagged a brace and Paul Warne and Chris Porter completed the scoring. Manager Ronnie Moore used the game to experiment and he put out different teams for both halves. San Jose had lost 5-0 the previous night to Wycombe Wanderers that meant that Athletic's round-robin meeting with Wycombe on 7th July would determine which team would win the cup. The final against Wycombe was played at SD Portmany's ground on July 7th 2005. Athletic had taken West Bromwich Albion and Republic of Ireland goalkeeper Joe Murphy with them on trial but he only lasted 20 minutes and had to be replaced by Les Pogliacomi. Oldham took the lead in the eighth minute with a fine goal from Paul Warne but Roger Johnson headed home the leveller for the Chairboys midway through the second half to take the game straight into a penalty shoot-out. Wycombe keeper Steve Williams was the hero of the day as he saved three out of the Latics' first four spot kicks to help Wycombe to a 3-1 shoot-out success. Athletic did, however, return home with a trophy as their trialist Andy Todd finished top scorer in the San-An Cup competition with three goals, courtesy of his hat-trick in the first game against local part-timers, San Jose. Latics manager Ronnie Moore commented; "I have been delighted with their attitude. They have had to endure some very hard training sessions in difficult conditions but they never once wavered in their commitment."

PLAYER OF THE YEAR

Some of the favourite players to grace Boundary Park have been awarded the prestigious accolade of Player of the Year. Many of the recipients have been goalkeepers and one of the first was ever-popular David Best, who was voted Player of the Year for 1967/68. Fellow shot-stopper Chris Ogden won the award in 1974/75 and another goalkeeper was recognised as the most outstanding when Andy Goram swept the votes for the 1982/83 season. Gary Kelly walked away with the Player of the Year trophy for 1996-97. Outfield player winners include Tommy Bryceland who was voted Player of the Year for 1970/71, Tony Carrs took a clean sweep of all the Player of the Year awards in 2000/01 while David Eyres won the sponsor's Player of the Season award. Paul Warne won the fans' Player of the Year award for 2006/07.

RECORD NUMBER OF WINS

York City came to Boundary Park on March 12th 1974 and an amazing 15,871 people showed up to see if the Latics could achieve their tenth consecutive league win – and they did not disappoint. Two goals from Maurice Whittle, one a penalty, were enough to see off York 2-1 and create a piece of history for the club. The run began with a 2-1 win at Wrexham on January 12th. A 3-2 home success over Halifax Town was followed by three successive away wins over AFC Bournemouth, Tranmere Rovers and Rochdale. A Maurice Whittle penalty and an Alan Groves goal were enough to brush aside Aldershot and another Groves marker at Blackburn Rovers – then wins over Cambridge United and Walsall – set them up for the York clash. Unfortunately, the Latics lost their next game at Chesterfield, 1-0.

SCOTLAND TOUR

The 1969 pre-season games were in Scotland. They began on August 2nd when goals from Jim Beardall (2) and Reg Blore were enough to see off East Stirling by 3-1. Two days later the team lost 3-2 at East Fife with the Latics goals coming from Derek Spence and Les Chapman. The tour was concluded on August 6th at Arbroath where Ian Wood and Jimmy Fryatt found the net in a 2-0 victory.

DON'T GET SHIRTY

Shirt sponsors play an integral part of any football team's financial balance sheet and big money is commonplace in today's world of high business football clubs. The first shirt sponsors of Oldham Athletic were Redsure and first appeared on November 11th 1980 in the 1-0 victory over Blackburn Rovers at Boundary Park. Redsure Electrical Limited was an electric motor overhauler and rewinder company which was based locally in Denton. The company was founded by lifelong Latics fan and marketing director Eric Redfern. The full list of subsequent shirt makers and sponsors since that date is listed below:

Season	Maker	Sponsor
1979/1980	Umbro	None
1980/1981	Umbro	Redsure
1981/1983	Umbro	None
1984/1985	Le Coq Sportif	None
1985/1987	Spall	Lees
1987/1988	Umbro	Martins Motor Group
1988/1989	Umbro	Lees Brewery & Maxwell
1989/1991	Umbro	Bovis
1991/1992	Umbro	Bovis
1992/1993	Umbro	JD Sports
1993/1995	Umbro	JD Sports
1995/1996	Umbro	JD Sports
1996/1998	Pony	JD Sports
1998/1999	Pony	Slumberland
1999/2000	Pony	Slumberland
2000/2001	Sparta	Slumberland
2001/2002	Sparta	Torex Foundation
2002/2003	Sparta	Torex Foundation
2002/2003	Sparta	Horners Motor Group

The deal with the Horners Motor Group was struck in the week before the start of the 2002/03 season. Supporters were so incensed at the way Chris Moore had devastated the club and, as only Torex shirts were available, a patch was sewn over the Torex logo that had the Horners logo printed on it. Individual supporters also blanked out the existing Torex logos on their shirts as a statement of their dissatisfaction at the way that Moore had systematically stripped their club of its best assets.

2002/2003	Carlotti	Horners Motor Group
2003/2004	Sparta	Horners Motor Group
2004/2005	Carlotti	Horners Motor Group
2005/2006	Carlotti	Horners Motor Group & Carlotti
2006/2007	Carlotti	Hillstone Developments
2007/2008	Carlotti	Hillstone Developments
2008/2009	Carlotti/Carbrini	JD Sports

PRACTICE MATCHES

In days long ago people lived for their Saturday football. The gates were bigger as can be proved by the fact that Athletic used to charge supporters for watching the team take part in practice matches. On August 16th 1919, 2,200 fans turned up and paid £35 7s 0d for the privilege of watching a practice match. In a similar game on August 15th 1922 an amazing total of 7,848 people paid to watch the game.

MELLOR v HOWE

In the 1925/26 season records were kept of directors' attendances at first team, reserves and Lancashire Mid-Week League fixtures for both home and away games. Athletic had 12 directors on their books and R. Mellor was the best attendee with 65 matches, whereas T. Howe only attended ten fixtures. In the 1927/28 season the directors' attendances followed a similar trend as R. Mellor attended 64 games and T. Howe only attended nine.

THE WEDDING HUNTER

Allan Hunter, 21-years-old at the time of the 1967 tour of Rhodesia and Malawi, had to return a day earlier than the remainder of the travelling party as he was due back home in Coleraine, Northern Ireland. His hurried return was due to an appointment on July 11th to get married to his fiancé, short-hand typist Carol Hegarty. He arrived home with less than 18 hours to spare to prepare for his nuptials.

I'LL HUFF AND I'LL PUFF

The Chaddy Road End stand was partly blown down due to the heavy January gales in 1964. The stand housed approximately 12,000 fans and it is a little known fact that it was also blown down during the course of its construction on October 28th 1928.

UPHILL OR DOWNHILL?

Before the finances from the Ford Sporting League in 1971, the slope on the ground from the Rochdale Road End to the Chadderton Road End was an amazing 6ft 4½ ins. When the Ford Sporting Stand was eventually built with the winnings, the bulldozers stepped in to level out the playing field.

POWER CRISIS GAME

Athletic's marathon third round FA Cup game with Cambridge United in the 1973/74 promotion season captured everybody's imagination. The country was in a power crisis caused by the miners' dispute and the Labour Government had imposed three-day working weeks to maintain some form of stability. This hit Athletic and the first replay at Boundary Park had to be played in the afternoon due to the fact that the power cuts forbade them the use of their floodlights. Even so the game attracted in excess of 10,000 fans.

APPRENTICES COINCIDENCES

At the conclusion of the 2008/09 season Athletic selected their budding footballers for the following season. A total of nine first-year apprentices were selected by youth team chief Tony Philliskirk and his staff and the lucky players joined the club for pre-season training in June. Some confusion could be experienced, though, as two of the youngsters share the same name. They are both called Matthew Carr. They will officially be distinguished as Matthew A. Carr and Matthew D. Carr, but to further complicate the situation they both play in the same position – central midfield!

FA CUP SEMI-FINAL 1989/90

The FA Cup semi-final against Manchester United was watched by 44,026 people at Maine Road as well as many millions more around the world as it was beamed to 26 countries by television. What an entertaining game it turned out to be. It was played on April 8th and Second Division Athletic had battled their way to the match with their First Division neighbours after some remarkable earlier performances. It was United's 18th appearance at this stage but it was only the second time that the Latics had reached an FA Cup semi-final, their only other appearance being back in 1913. It had been suggested that Athletic's artificial pitch had given them an unfair advantage and had helped them to reach this stage but there was nothing artificial about the performance that they put in against United on this day. Athletic won the first corner of the match in the sixth minute and Rick Holden took the kick that came back out to him. He drove the ball hard and low back into the danger area and Earl Barrett shocked United by giving the Latics an early lead with a simple tap in. In the 29th minute Steve Bruce won the ball off Ritchie on the halfway line and passed to Neil Webb who threaded the ball through to England captain Bryan Robson. Robson beat Jon Hallworth with his shot and although he got a hand to it he couldn't prevent the ball from going over the line for the equaliser. The deadlock was broken again in the 71st minute when United took the lead for the first time through Webb who knew little about the goal as it bounced off his head and landed over the line. Another turn of events occurred just four minutes later when never-say-die Athletic scored yet again. Irwin sent Neil Redfearn away on the right and his centre was met by Marshall who smashed home a low volley that found the bottom corner of the net to send the many thousands of Latics fans into rapture. With the score at 2-2, the game went to extra time and the Reds scored through Wallace when he beat Hallworth with a low shot. In the 107th minute of the game, Marshall set off on a gangling run down the left wing. He centred the ball and Roger Palmer ghosted in at the far post to steer the ball home from close range to force a replay, although it could have still gone either way.

BILLY URMSON

Billy Urmson was Athletic's youth team coach for 27 years and in February 2003 was asked to step down from his role. His assistant, David Cross, was also part of the redundancy package. Billy was born in Little Lever, Bolton. He joined Bury as an amateur in 1955 at the age of 16. He subsequently played at Stockport County and Caernarvon but the turning point came when he joined Alan Ball Senior at Nantwich, for it was through him that he became involved and interested in coaching. Indeed, he was Alan Ball's demonstrator when the World Cup-winner ran courses. A return spell at Bury as youth, then first team, coach was followed by three years as manager of Horwich RMI before he was 'headhunted' to come and coach the youngsters at Boundary Park in 1974. Before turning full-time, Billy was once a French polisher and some of this art must have rubbed off on him to make him the smooth-finished talker he is – at least to the office staff. As a tribute to the sterling work that Billy did, the following acknowledgements are from the people he knew and worked with:

Oldham chief executive Alan Hardy: "My heartfelt gratitude goes to Bill Urmson. These redundancies are something we would have liked to avoid. But, due to increasing financial pressures it was necessary that economies were made through all departments, including coaching, as well as the recent redundancies from players, administration and groundstaff."

Former chairman Ian H. Stott: "Perhaps the youth team may think otherwise when they are assailed by a voice that needs no assistance from a loud hailer. But, we all know his bark is worse than his bite. He thinks of Carl Valentine and Wayne Harrison and can point to the fact that Mike Milligan, Nick Henry, Andy Barlow, Paul Bernard and Paul Gerrard all featured in the first-team squad, having survived the Billy Urmson academy."

Oldham Chronicle reporter Tony Bugby: "Bill now proudly boasts of being the longest serving member of the Latics' backroom staff. Terry McDermott, guided by Bill at Bury, was arguably the player who went on to achieve the greatest success with Newcastle United, Liverpool and England, winning 25 caps and being named Footballer of the Year. Bill estimates that at least 30 of his young trainees have gone on to make a living as full-time professionals."

By a strange twist of fate, Urmson was re-appointed as a scout by John Sheridan's successor Joe Royle in March 2009.

SCOREBOARDS DON'T LIE

Athletic recorded the biggest ever League Cup win when they beat Scarborough 7-0 in the third round in the 1989/90 season. Frankie Bunn got six goals on that famous night and after his final goal went in, in the 89th minute, the scoreboard read Bunn 6 Scarborough 0!

FA CUP SEMI-FINAL REPLAY 1993/94

A poor performance in the replay at Maine Road on April 13th 1994 ended Athletic's aspirations and their dream of a final appearance would remain just that. Athletic had previously been beaten semi-finalists by Manchester United and it didn't take long for the continuing pattern to emerge. Ex-Latics full-back Denis Irwin was the first to strike as early as the ninth minute as he rifled home a typical Irwin goal. Andrei Kanchelskis returned to the United team after suspension and it was he who went on to torment the Latics defence. He scored the Reds' second goal after an amazing solo run that ended with him hammering past Jon Hallworth. Several chances did fall to Athletic but, unfortunately, they had left their shooting boots at home, although Neil Pointon continued his scoring run against United with a close range shot in the 40th minute after Darren Beckford had flicked on Rick Holden's corner. In the second half, Hallworth uncharacteristically dropped a Ryan Giggs corner and Bryan Robson scrambled the ball over the line. Kanchelskis set up Giggs for United's fourth in the 67th minute with a goal that totally killed the game dead leaving no chance of any Athletic fightback. The dream was over and it culminated in a disastrous run of results, with the Latics' failing to win any of their remaining seven fixtures of the season. A month later they were relegated from the Premier League after three seasons in the top flight. It is still argued by many Oldham fans that the team never recovered from *That Mark Hughes Goal*.

ALL CHANGE AT BARROW

The Latics played at Barrow in a Third Division (North) game on September 14th 1957 and only one player was selected who had taken part in the previous game, a 4-1 loss at Hartlepools United. Outside-right Ron Fawley was the lucky player who kept his place.

LATICS MUNICH LINK

Ex-Latics player Colin Whittaker, who played for the club between 1962-64 and scored 29 goals in 72 league appearances, was a true 'wizard of the wing' who scored over one hundred goals in his footballing career, including eight hat-tricks. A wonderful trapper of the ball, Colin played for Sheffield Wednesday, Shrewsbury Town, QPR and Rochdale, before moving to Oldham. After leaving the Latics he played at Barrow and became player-manager at Stalybridge Celtic. Colin tells the following strange tale: "I was playing at Oldham in 1964 when I damaged my cartilage and I ended up going to Old Trafford for treatment where I got to know Sir Matt Busby. I got up off a treatment table and started to hobble on one leg, so Sir Matt told me to take the crutches he'd used when he left hospital in Munich. I used them for about a month before putting them in my garage. It never entered my head how important they might be until the 40th anniversary of the Munich crash, when I offered the crutches to United for a display in the club museum." Now retired, Colin spends six months of the year on Spain's Costa Del Sol.

HONOURS

Premier League: Founder Members 1992/1993
First Division Runners-up 1914/1915
Second Division Runners-up 1909/1910
Second Division Champions..1990/1991
Third Division (North) Champions..1952/1953
Third Division Champions...1973/1974
Fourth Division Runners-up..1962/1963
FA Cup Semi-finalists 1912/13, 1989/90, 1993/94
League Cup Finalists 1989/90
Associate Members Northern Section Finalists 2004/05
Associate Members Northern Section Semi-finalists 2001/02
Lancashire Senior Cup Winners................. 1907/08, 1966/67, 2005/06
Ford Sporting League Winners 1970/71
Sir Fred Pontin Gold Cup six-a-side winners 1978
Anglo-Scottish Cup finalists...1978/79

JOBSON ALMOST GAVE UP

Richard Jobson, whose fee of £460,000 equalled the record paid for David Currie in the same month of August 1990, almost gave up his playing career. When he was a teenager playing for Burton Albion he was also studying a civil engineering course at Nottingham University. As he did not have transport, he had to rely on his teammates to give him a lift for the 30 miles to training. The stress was tremendous but he persevered and was rewarded with a £15,000 offer from Watford manager Graham Taylor, who later went on to coach England. The offer was huge by comparison to what he was earning in the semi-professional game. Circumstances at Vicarage Road meant that he was playing in the First Division, albeit on the left wing and not his central defensive role. He commented, "I think they put me on the wing so I could be least trouble there."

INTER-LEAGUE GAME

Boundary Park was the venue for an England v Ireland game in 1910. The result was a resounding 8-1 victory for England.

"I HAVE TO GET STRAIGHT OFF!"

When Rick Holden returned to Boundary Park for his second spell with Athletic in 1994 he had got into the habit of not doing any warm-ups prior to the games. The reason was two-fold: one was that he was doing so much running that he decided to conserve energy by staying in the dressing room; two was that he was suffering from a long and heavy cold so he opted for a warm bath, a read of the programme and a cup of tea to try to keep warm. Paul Gerrard was the Latics' young goalkeeper who observed Rick undergoing this strange ritual. Gerrard asked him why he was having a bath before the game. Rick, knowing him to be, let's say, 'not the brightest bulb in the chandelier' told him that he had a wedding reception to go to straight after the game and to save time he was having his wash prior to the game. The young keeper then went and told all the lads in the dressing room who as you can well imagine fell about the place laughing.

ATHLETIC'S ALLITERATES

A collection of current and former Latics players with names beginning with the same first and second initials.

Alfred Agar
George Greenall
Bert Blackshaw
Harold Houlahan
Bill Baldwin
Harry Haslam
Bill Blackshaw
Harry Horrocks
Billy Boswell
Henry Hancock
Billy Bottomley
John Jarvis
Bill Bradbury
John Jones
Billy Broadbent
Ken Knighton
Ben Brelsford
Kevin McCurley
Ben Bunting
Mike Milligan
Ben Burgess
Peter Phoenix
Ben Burrage
Percival 'Roy' Player
Brian Birch
Simon Stainrod
Charles Campbell
Stan Smith
Clifton Chadwick
Ted Taylor
David Davies
William Waite
David 'Dickie' Down

William Walsh
Fred Flavell
William Wood
Frederick Fitton
Wilkin Ward

FIRST PLAYER OF THE YEAR

Bob Ledger was the recipient of the club's first-ever Player of the Year award which was given out in 1967.

FAMOUS NAMES

When 'The Three Amigos' opted to buy cash-strapped, and in administration, Oldham Athletic in 2003, they looked carefully at the playing squad and were surprised to see such prestigious names such as Zola, Roca, Owen, Schumacher and O'Halloran on the list. Little were they to know that they were not about to inherit the likes of Gianfranco, William, Michael, Harald and Stephen. Instead they took on Calvin, Carlos, Gareth, Stephen and Matt but to this day they must still live with the thought that their team could have been so much more valuable if they had bought the players that they thought they had.

WEATHER TO CHANGE OR NOT?

Crewe Alexandra were the visitors to Oldham for an FA Cup replay on 13th December 1949, a game which resulted in a 0-0 draw. It needed a second replay before Athletic won through by a 3-0 scoreline but the pitch and weather on that day meant that Athletic went through 24 pairs of shorts and 26 jerseys to complete the match.

COMMEMORATIVE TROPHY

A commemorative trophy was awarded to Athletic on their visit to Great Dyke as part of the Rhodesia and Malawi tour in 1967. It reads: Great Dyke and Lomagimdi. Presented to OAFC on the occasion of their visit to the Great Dyke 1-7-67 and it still resides in the Athletic trophy cabinet at Boundary Park.

MANNION FOR OLDHAM

Athletic's shareholders put the club under pressure in 1947 when they requested that they sign Wilf Mannion from Middlesbrough. The England player was available for the huge fee of £25,000, and director and former chairman Arthur Barlow offered the club a £2,000 interest-free loan on the proviso that another 15 supporters would do the same. Many supporters in the town made collections in a combined effort to help the deal go through but, unfortunately, they never raised enough and the deal didn't materialise. Questions were asked for many years about whatever happened to all the money collected.

WALES INTERNATIONALS

The following Latics players have represented Wales at international level but not necessarily while they were on Oldham's books.

Evan Jones	1911-12	7 caps
David Davies	1912-13	2 caps
Bill Goodwin	1913-21 & 1925-26	2 victory internationals
Charlie Jones	1923-25	7caps
Albert Gray	1923-27	24 caps and 1 WL XI app
Charlie Butler	1935-36	schoolboy
'Taffy' Jones	1935-39	junior
John Jones	1948-49	schoolboy
Jack Warner	1951-52	2 caps
Frank Scrine	1953-56	2 caps
Derek Williams	1956-59	amateur
Brian Jarvis	1961-63	youth
Reg Blore	1965-70	U-23
Stephen Morgan	1987	schoolboy and youth
Andy Holden	1989-92	1 cap
Mathew Tipton	1994-2002	U-18 and U-21
Josh Low	2002-03	U-21
Gareth Owen	2004 & 2005-06	youth
Neal Eardley	2006-present	U-21 and 10 caps
Craig Davies	2007-09	U-21 and 5 caps
Mark Crossley	2007-09	'B' level and 8 caps

TIME FOR RECOGNITION

John Ryan was presented with a carriage clock in May 1983 to commemorate his first international game for England under-21s.

LUCKY 7

Ex-Everton player Neil Adams could be nicknamed 'Lucky 7' as he had a remarkable record in the number seven shirt. In February 1991, he had been named 11 times in the starting line-up and the team had won 10 and drawn the other game. The previous season he wore the number seven shirt in 30 games and the team lost just four; one of the games was the League Cup final against Nottingham Forest.

FANTASTIC ON THE PLASTIC

Athletic travelled to Loftus Road on November 24th 1981 to play on Queens Park Rangers' new artificial pitch. The 0-0 draw became significant as they were the first team ever to not concede a goal in a game on the surface. The tail end of a galeforce wind, typical Oldham weather, were the conditions that Athletic endured in the first ever game to be played on the new artificial surface at Boundary Park on August 25th 1986. Rather than playing on a lush carpet, the fibrilated polypropolyne pitch looked more like a beach than a football field due to all the sand necessary to help it bed in. Gone was the famous 6ft 4½ ins. slope which used to incline down to the Chaddy End as it had been levelled with the changes to the pitch. Barnsley were the visitors for the first home match of the new season and goals from Nick Henry and Roger Palmer were enough to see off their Yorkshire rivals. The last match ever to be played on the synthetic field was a testimonial game for all-time leading marksman Palmer. It was played against Manchester City on May 14th 1991 and Palmer scored the second goal in a 3-2 victory over the visitors. The pitch was ripped up after the game and the loss of the surface cost Athletic an estimated £50,000 per season in lost revenue from community use. The Taylor Report was responsible for the change as new league regulations stated that the top two divisions would not be allowed to use artificial surfaces. An estimated cost of £200,000 for replacement combined with £1m in further upgrades to the ground meant that the Latics would need to find other sources of income for their new season in the top flight.

URI GELLER'S INTEREST IN ATHLETIC

After much publicity in the late 1990s regarding various attempts to take control over the club's affairs, Uri Geller, the famous spoon bender, had shown some interest and went into great depth about how his techniques and methods have moved people beyond their expectations and imaginations by seizing control of their lives and imposing their dreams on the world. Unfortunately, it didn't help by allowing him to seize control of Oldham Athletic AFC and impose on the dreams of thousands of Latics followers. Uri confided that, although the Latics idea fell through, he is still searching for the 'right club' but emphasises that when it does come along it has to come from the heart. Uri concluded that it was a hard life for all Oldham Athletic supporters. At that time the supporters had seen their side slide from being in arguably the most prestigious and competitive football league in the world, to a relegation spot and heading for the third division, just one step up from non-league football with automatic relegation for the bottom club. Thankfully, things eventually took a swing in the right direction and Oldham fans can once again look forward to a brighter future with less doom and gloom.

MATCH PREPARATION

On New Year's Eve 1989 Jon Hallworth attended a house party and, as he wasn't supposed to be in the squad for the match at Leeds United on New Year's Day 1990, maybe he had a drink or two too many. In the circumstances he wasn't too bad and he was eventually put to bed. The following morning he received a phone call to say that Andy Rhodes was unable to play and that the substitute goalkeeper wasn't ready either. Jon was told he was playing. After having several black coffees poured down him he was dropped off at the ground at around eleven o'clock. Unbelievably, Hallworth had one of his best games for the club and he performed heroics in the deserved 1-1 draw at Elland Road. After the game he confessed that he was still hazy at the warm-up but soon sobered up when John Hendrie fired a rasping shot at him after just thirty seconds of the game. Jon and his mate Gary Williams were after-match regulars in the Horton Arms in Royton.

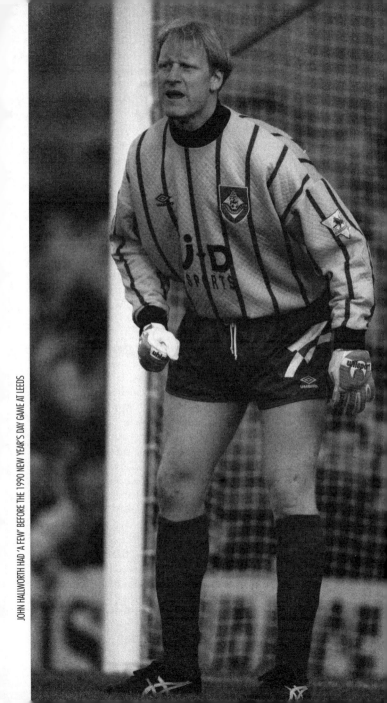

FIVE PLAYERS WITH 200 APPEARANCES

Ian Robins made his 200th appearance for Athletic as they took on Chelsea in a 0-0 draw at Boundary Park on April 19th 1977. The Latics team on that day contained no fewer than five players who had made the magical number of 200 appearances. Leading the list was record-breaking Ian Wood with 408, followed by Maurice Whittle (305), Ronnie Blair (232) and David Shaw (207).

LAST POST AND A SPITFIRE AT BOUNDARY PARK

It was an emotional day at Boundary Park on April 14th 1945 as 857 supporters held a minute's silence in the pouring rain in respect for President Roosevelt who had died the previous day. As the last post was played a Spitfire overhead dipped in salute. Centre-forward Cottrill put the Latics ahead minutes into the game and they went on to beat Tranmere Rovers 2-1. The previous week the Latics had suffered a 7-1 reverse against the Rovers at Prenton Park.

CHAMPIONSHIP-WINNING GAME 1991

In one of the most remarkable and memorable games ever staged at Boundary Park, Sheffield Wednesday came to spoil the party for championship-seeking Athletic on May 11th 1991. It was the last day of the season and West Ham United were in top spot, Athletic were second and Wednesday occupied third spot. To make it even more interesting, the Hammers were entertaining fourth-placed Notts County. West Ham United lost 2-1 at home to County but as news filtered through to Upton Park that Athletic were losing 2-0 at home the celebrations began. Athletic remarkably pulled back the score to 2-2 in regulation time but even a draw was enough to give the Hammers the trophy. With all other games ended, referee Vic Callow allowed some extra time to compensate for Wednesday's time-wasting antics. After 92 minutes of pulsating football, John Sheridan brought down Andy Barlow for a penalty to the home side. The penalty became the last kick of the last game on the last day of the season. It just couldn't have been scripted. Neil Redfearn stepped up to take the kick but then the referee stopped the kick to book a Sheffield player. It all added to the tension. Cool as a cucumber Redfearn strode up to plant the penalty – his most important goal ever – home and to send Boundary Park into a frenzy of celebration. Fans invaded the pitch to celebrate and in true World Cup-style commentary they thought it was all over – well, it was now! Athletic were back in the big time after a break of 68 years. The championship trophy arrived by courier at Boundary Park with West Ham's name engraved on it, much to the embarrassment of league officials. The top of the table was as follows:

	P	W	D	L	F	A	W	D	L	F	A	Pts	GD
Oldham Athletic	46	17	5	1	55	21	8	8	7	28	32	88	+30
West Ham United	46	15	6	2	41	18	9	9	5	19	16	87	+26
Sheffield Weds	46	12	10	1	43	23	10	6	7	37	28	82	+29
Notts County	46	14	4	5	45	28	9	7	7	31	27	80	+21

THAT'S MY SEAT

When Michael Clegg used to travel to away matches on the team coach he always had to sit on the same seat, which was on the last set.

YOU SOLD HOW MANY?

Northwich Victoria had drawn Athletic at home in the FA Cup on January 29th 1977, but when they discovered that they had sold more tickets than their capacity could hold they were forced to change the venue to Maine Road, Manchester. Athletic won the tie 3-1. Two goals from Vic Halom and one from Carl Valentine were enough to see off the non-league team in front of 28,635 supporters.

BIG WIN – RECORD SCORER

Athletic entertained Chester at Boundary Park in arctic-like conditions on January 19th 1952. Sixteen-year-old Eddie Hopkinson, who went on to play for Bolton Wanderers and England, made two early blunders to set Chester up with a 2-1 lead within the first half-hour of the game but it was 30-year-old Eric Gemmell who took the glory from the match. In an amazing turnaround, Gemmell hit seven goals (six in succession), a record for any Oldham player, as the Latics went on to win the game 11-2 in front of 13,458 delirious supporters.

BANGLADESHI TOUR

Athletic sent its under-20 team to play three matches in Bangladesh in May 2007 and became the first-ever professional football club from the UK to play in the country. The president of the Bangladeshi Football Federation (BFF), Mr. S. A. Sultan said; "To find the prosperous future of Bangladeshi players, we want long-term relationships with Oldham. This will help both of us develop good relationships between Bangladesh and the UK." The trip was organised to cement ties and was also a chance for potential young players from Bangladesh to take part in extensive training at the Oldham Academy. Throughout the tour, the Latics players and officials were greeted as VIPs and there was huge media interest with reporters constantly pressuring the team for stories and interviews. The two matches held in the capital were televised live by satellite channel ATN Bangla and crowds flocked to watch:

7th May v Mohammedan Sporting Club at the Bangabandhu National Stadium, Dhaka: Around three thousand supporters watched the hosts win a 2-1 game with Matty Barlow scoring the lone consolation goal for the Latics when he tapped in from a Dean Smalley cross. Oldham made nine substitutions at half-time as the scorching heat took its toll on the youngsters. After the game Tony Philliskirk commented; "It was a good game and both sides wasted chances. Mohammedan played well and I have to admit that my boys were really undone by the conditions. It was too hot and humid and the players were tired after a long trip. We know what to do and hope to settle it by our next match."

10th May v Bangladesh under-23s in Sylhet: Mike Pearson crashed home a fine strike after 15 minutes as the Latics earned a hard-fought draw. The hosts equalised just before the break but Oldham were the better side and created enough opportunities to win the game. The temperature was a baking 39 degrees and director Ian Hill described the lads as, "an absolute credit to the club". The attendance was assessed at somewhere between the estimated 6,000 to anything up to the official gate of 15,000 spectators.

12th May v Abahani Ltd, Dhaka at the Bangabandhu National Stadium, Dhaka: The last exhibition game of the tour resulted in a 0-0 draw, although the encounter was full of excitement. The home side dominated most of the proceedings but failed to convert any of their chances into goals, much to the disappointment of the local fans in the big bowl.

LOWEST AWAY GATES

The lowest ever attendance in Athletic's venture into the Anglo-Italian Cup was set when a paltry 311 fans turned out to watch the game in Ancona on September 5th 1995. The record for a Third Division (North) League game was 1,490 in a game that was played at New Brighton's Tower ground on February 29th 1936 which the Latics won 3-1 with goals from Arthur Buckley (2) and Bill Walsh. In the Third Division (North) Cup game at Southport on March 9th 1937 only 800 supporters decided to put in an appearance. The League Cup tie at Workington on August 26th 1975 was viewed by only 1,462 spectators who watched a George Jones hat-trick seal a 3-0 win for the Latics. The worst-supported Fourth Division game came in a 2-0 loss at Gateshead on April 23rd 1960 when 1,492 attended the game. The FA Cup record was gained in an enthralling match at Formby on January 6th 1973 when 3,000 fans, many from Oldham, crammed into the tiny Brows Lane ground. The home side had rented a stand to accommodate the visiting supporters and some fans spent most of the game chanting, "Rent-a-Stand, Rent-a-Stand".

I'M SICK OF THIS

Poor Andy Linighan. The tall centre-back – who was one of the many cut-price players that Athletic took off the hands of Leeds United – harboured a little known fear. The fact was that he was always physically sick five minutes before he entered the field for the game.

UNDERGROUND HEATING

In 1980 Athletic joined the few teams that had installed underground heating under their pitch. Lottery money added to funds raised by local businesses allowed work on the 'Meltaway' soil-warming system beginning in the middle of May. The Swedish system cost £60,000 and used an oil-fired boiler and 16 miles of plastic cable to prevent the pitch freezing by circulating water at a temperature of 20 degrees. It took until early December before the heating was ready for use. Granges Essom undertook the total installation of the system, which was run under the existing gas supply.

TELEVISED GAMES

The Latics have appeared many times on television. Granada TV televised the 1-0 home win against Blackpool on January 15th 1977. The advent of First Division football in 1992/93 meant that six of the Latics games were to be shown live on TV. The first round FA Cup game at Chasetown on November 6th 2005 was televised live. Little Chasetown were seven leagues and 133 positions below Athletic but it needed a David Eyres equalising goal to bring the minnows back to Boundary Park. The replay was also shown on TV but the Latics easily won by 4-0 with goals from Paul Warne, Chris Porter (2) and Chris Hall. Athletic's second round FA Cup tie at King's Lynn on December 1st 2006 was also televised. The Latics won 2-0 with goals from Chris Porter and Chris Hall. Two games were shown for the 2008/09 season. The 0-0 draw at league leaders Leicester City was screened by Sky TV on February 7th and the 1-1 draw at home to Leeds United on March 2nd was also a live game.

SIGNIFICANT GAMES

Athletic suffered their 1,000th league defeat in the 1978/79 season. When Jim Steel scored the only goal of the game at Boundary Park to see off neighbours Blackburn Rovers on November 11th 1980, the win was Oldham's 1,000th which was achieved in front of 7,748 supporters. The 3,000th league game played by Athletic was played on May 7th 1988 when AFC Bournemouth were the visitors to Boundary Park. A penalty from Andy Ritchie, combined with an own goal, gave the Latics a 2-0 victory. Oldham's 4000th goal was scored by Paul Heaton on 19th December 1981 in a Second Division game against Orient, a match which the Latics won 3-2.

SPORTS HALL

In 1980 grants of £60,000 and £20,000 were received from the football grounds improvement trust, and the sports council, respectively, towards the cost of building the sports hall at Boundary Park. The hall has since been demolished to make way for the new Boundary Park refurbishment.

FA CUP SEMI-FINAL REPLAY 1989/90

The replay took place on April 11th at the home of Manchester City in a repeat of the first meeting. The tie carried on much the same as the first game which had more twists and turns than the famous Snake Pass over the Pennines. Ian Marshall intercepted a Pallister back-pass in the first minute and almost gave the Latics a sensational opening goal but his shot from an acute angle was just wide. Next Andy Ritchie brought a good save out of Leighton with a 20-yarder which stung the keeper's hands. Disaster struck Oldham as Marshall had to retire with a thigh injury and Paul Warhurst came on to deputise. There was no doubting that the Latics would miss the aerial presence of Marshall and it was United who took the lead in the 50th minute with a simple tap in from McClair, a goal reminiscent of the final equaliser from Roger Palmer in the last meeting. Leighton was forced to make a crucial save from Mike Milligan but Athletic were not going to give in and they were rewarded with just ten minutes of the game left. A right wing Rick Holden centre was smashed into the roof of the net by Ritchie, a goal which sent the game amazingly, once again, to extra time. The Latics fans were certainly getting value for money in a season which had been littered with extra-time contests. In added time Holden centred for Neil Redfearn but his header was fractionally wide. The game was sealed in the 110th minute when the adventurous play of Athletic finally took its toll. Ironically, the goal was scored by local boy Ian Robbins who had previously played for Boundary Park Juniors – a cruel twist of fate. The Latics never gave up though and Ritchie had another effort flicked wide by Leighton and his last-minute cross was just too far back for Palmer to capitalise. United held on and were very relieved to hear the final whistle. Athletic had lost the tie but they had won the hearts of football fans the world over with their adventurous and cavalier style of play. The real winner on the day was football itself as both teams had played both legs in a sporting and well-spirited manner. Neutral fans would have found it difficult to distinguish which side was the First Division outfit in this enthralling saga which was now, unfortunately for Athletic, finally over.

CLUB SHOP

The first club shop was used in March 1976 after Athletic agreed to rent 61, Hollins Road for £10 a week to advertise the club and sell souvenirs.

WE'RE NOT QUITE READY YET!

When Athletic played Leeds City on November 30th 1907 the half-time score was 1-1 but the Latics were late coming back onto the field. The referee blew his whistle two or three times so he allowed Leeds to kick off towards the Rochdale Road end. Captain Jimmy Fay saw what was happening and raced down the steps to the field to give chase on the Leeds winger Croot but he couldn't stop him centring for Gemmell to score. Oldham eventually won the game 4-2.

DJ

Franny Ward left the club in August 1981 to become the promotions manager at Oldham Rugby and Alan Stone came in as cover as the match-day DJ. However, Ward is now back in residence at Boundary Park.

OVAL BALLS

Today, the Latics share their ground with the Oldham Roughyeds rugby team but the first rugby game ever played on Boundary Park took place on January 10th 1982. With the rugby ground completely frozen over, Oldham Rugby took full advantage of Athletic's undersoil heating and played their home game against Batley at Boundary Park. Oldham ran out victorious and won the game 17-9.

PLAYER DIES ON FIELD

The first Latics-related player to die during a first-team game was Sam Wynne. On April 30th 1927, former Athletic player Wynne collapsed in the game at Bury, who were entertaining Sheffield United. He died in the dressing room and the postmortem revealed that he was suffering from pneumonia. The game was abandoned and replayed with all receipts going to Wynne's widow. Wynne only joined Athletic by a fluke. Manager Herbert Bamlett was scheduled to watch a game at Ellesmere Port Town but arrived early. He was persuaded to take in the Wirrall Cup Final which was being played at Port Sunlight. He spotted Wynne playing for Neston Colliery and signed him after the game up in the team bath.

DE LA SALLE COLLEGE

Athletic had to pay De La Salle College, Middleton the sum of £1,100 for the use of their training facilities for the 1979/80 season. The club used the college for some time but decided to discontinue the practice after the 1981/82 season due to financial reasons. The decision was made that the £2,250, plus travelling expenses, was just too much for the Latics to continue with the exercise.

WAGES

When Jimmy Faye's first contract was signed on May 13th 1905, he received £1 10s 0d per week plus travelling expenses. Jack Dyson was a part-time coach and was awarded a pay rise in July 1973 – up to approximately £5/week. When the retained list for 1976 was released it was disclosed that Alan Groves was the club's best-paid player.

GROUND BOMBED

A pre-Christmas air raid in 1941 left Athletic with a devastated ground and a huge repair bill of £671. Damage to the ground included the main stand being left in disarray with every window in the offices being shattered.

IRELAND TOUR

Athletic ventured over the Irish Sea for their 1966 pre-season games. They played four games and came back undefeated. But they didn't have it all their own way. The first game was played on August 1st at Linfield and goals from Reg Blore and Frank Large gave the Latics a 2-2 draw. On August 3rd they went to Coleraine to fight out a 0-0 draw and a day later they achieved a third successive tie when Large and Ian Towers chipped in with goals to earn a 2-2 share of the game. Eric Magee played in the game against his soon-to-be employers. The tour was concluded in fine style on August 7th when Athletic beat Shelbourne 6-1. Billy Dearden, Large, a hat-trick from Towers and Jimmy McIlroy were the tormentors of the Shelbourne defence.

HIGHEST GATES ON NEUTRAL GROUNDS

In the FA Cup semi-final at Maine Road on April 8th 1990, 44,026 supporters set a record on neutral ground as Athletic and Manchester United fought out an exciting 3-3 draw after extra time. Athletic's first ever Wembley appearance against Nottingham Forest in the League Cup final on April 29th 1990 attracted 74,343 people and is the record number of supporters ever to watch the Latics play a match. Oldham lost the match 1-0 to a Nigel Jemson goal. An appearance at Wembley on April 10th 1994 in the FA Cup semi-final brought in 56,399 spectators and shattered the previous best FA Cup gate from four years prior. Yet again, the opposition was Manchester United, this time the teams played to a 1-1 draw.

INCLEMENT WEATHER

On November 29th 1919, Manchester United entertained Athletic in a First Division fixture. It was a very foggy day and the game was stopped 16 minutes from the end with the Latics winning 3-1. Gee, Jones and Hemsley scored the goals. Oldham welcomed Nottingham Forest to Boundary Park on December 15th 1928 but the match was abandoned owing to fog with the score at 2-1 for Forest. Dyson scored the Athletic goal. On February 25th 1933, and with a blizzard blowing and the pitch covered in snow, the home game against West Ham was postponed. Fog again disrupted a game on January 3rd 1934 as the 1-1 draw with Plymouth Argyle could not be followed owing to the thickness of the fog. Not many people in the ground saw Rowley score Athletic's goal. On January 21st 1936 the Midweek League match against Burnley 'A' was cancelled due to the ground being unfit. The cancellation also corresponded with the death of the king. The scheduled match on the following day at Crewe Alexandra was also cancelled due to a snow-covered field. The game at New Brighton on December 25th 1937 was abandoned at half-time on account of fog and two days later, the return fixture at Boundary Park was not commenced because of the continuing heavy fog. The Boxing Day match at home against Stockport County in 1938 was abandoned due to fog after 63 minutes with Athletic losing 1-0. On March 27th 1979 the home match against Burnley was postponed because of a waterlogged pitch.

MUSICAL LATICS

The Oldham Athletic playing squad sung along with local comedy duo Cannon and Ball to record a version of 'The Boys in Blue' song which was released prior to the Latics first-ever Wembley appearance in the League Cup final in 1990. The song was inspired from the duo's film with the same title. Unfortunately, the record didn't inspire the team to win as they went down 1-0 to Nottingham Forest. In 1991 the Latics Fanzine Beyond The Boundary released a single rap record entitled 'The Roger Rap'. On the reverse was a reggae version recorded by local Oldham band Introspect. The songs were dedicated to Latics hero Roger Palmer and were released during his testimonial season. Latics midfielder Lee Richardson, who was captured from Aberdeen, was also the member of a Scottish rock band called One God Universe and they released an album in 1994. Grandad Roberts and his son Elvis released a single in 1998 called 'Meat Pie Sausage Roll' that was based on an old tune that the Latics fans used to sing every time they got a corner. The fans would sing "Ooooh it's a corner" and the line was changed to "Ooooh – we got a corner" and formed the chorus of the catchy song.

AMATEUR PLAYERS

Throughout the 1934/35 season Oldham Athletic used a total of 20 professionals and 44 amateurs.

FIRST EVER GOALS

The first recorded goalscorer for Athletic (as Pine Villa) was Caffrey who scored one of the goals in a 4-0 win at Wellington United on October 2nd 1897. The game was an Oldham Junior Association League game. Caffrey's Christian name was never recorded, nor were the other goalscorers on the day. Billy Dodds scored the first ever Latics goal in the Football League. In the match report of the game at Stoke City on September 8th 1907 his goal in a 3-1 win was described as a "clinking" shot. Joe Shadbolt was credited with scoring the club's first ever goal in the FA Cup when Athletic beat Ashton Town 2-1 at home on October 7th 1905. In the inaugural season of the League Cup in the 1960/61 season, Brian Birch scored the first ever goal for Athletic in the competition. It came in a 2-1 win over Hartlepools United on October 11th; a game watched by 3,630 fans.

FIRST PROMOTION TO THE FIRST DIVISION

Athletic's meteoric rise up the leagues culminated in the 1909/10 season when they achieved promotion to the First Division. The season started badly with the Latics occupying bottom spot with just two points after the first five matches. When Jimmy Faye was promoted from defender to attacker, the Latics' fortunes changed and they went on a run of just one defeat in 21 matches. When they entertained Hull City on April 30th 1910 in the final league game of the season, they had won their previous five games and were undefeated in seven matches. They beat Hull City by a score of 3-0 and secured their first ever promotion to the elite of the First Division, albeit by goal difference, and ironically over Hull. The Boundary Park gate of 29,083 was a record and many of the club's ecstatic fans swarmed the field at the end to hail the conquering heroes. The end of season table was as follows:

	P	W	D	L	F	A	W	D	L	F	A	Pts	GAvg
Manchester City	38	15	2	2	51	17	8	6	5	30	23	54	.025
Oldham Athletic	38	15	2	2	47	9	8	5	6	32	30	53	.0256
Hull City	38	13	4	2	52	19	10	3	6	28	27	53	.7391
Derby County	38	15	2	2	46	15	7	7	5	26	32	53	.5319
Leicester City	38	15	2	2	60	20	5	2	12	19	38	44	.3620
Glossop North E	38	14	1	4	42	18	4	6	9	22	39	43	.1228
Fulham	38	9	7	3	28	13	5	6	8	23	30	41	.1860
Wolverhampton W	38	14	3	2	51	22	3	3	13	13	41	40	.0158
Barnsley	38	15	3	1	48	15	1	4	14	14	44	39	.0508
Bradford PA	38	12	1	6	47	28	5	3	11	17	31	38	.0847
West Brom Albion	38	8	5	6	30	23	8	0	11	28	33	37	.0357
Blackpool	38	7	7	5	24	18	7	1	11	26	34	36	.9615
Stockport County	38	9	6	4	37	20	4	2	13	13	27	34	.0638
Burnley	38	12	2	5	43	21	2	4	13	19	40	34	.0163
Lincoln City	38	7	6	6	27	24	3	5	11	15	45	31	.6086
Clapton Orient	38	10	4	5	26	15	2	2	15	11	45	30	.6166
Leeds City	38	8	4	7	30	33	2	3	14	16	47	27	.575
Gainsborough T	38	8	3	8	22	21	2	3	14	11	54	26	.44
Grimsby Town	38	8	3	8	31	19	1	3	15	19	58	24	.6493
Birmingham City	38	7	4	8	28	26	1	3	15	14	52	23	.5384

FLAG DAY

When the Latics won their way through to the FA Cup semi-finals in 1994 two of their fans, Stephen and Christine Earley, had a giant flag made to commemorate the occasion. The flag, which cost in the region of £2,500, measured 100ft by 50ft and was believed, at the time, to be the biggest in the country. It weighed 12 stone and needed four strong men to carry it when packed. It had to be specially fireproofed before it was allowed into Wembley Stadium for the game. The flag has a giant owl logo and the words "Keep The Faith" emblazoned across it and is now mothballed to be brought out just for special occasions.

ROUGH DIAMOND

Joe Royle was watching the Oldham reserve side play at Ashton United in a game circa 1984 and was raving about a scrawny-looking runt in the team who looked less like a professional footballer than anyone could even imagine. The youngster could not run, was too small, had no great ability, looked like he had been dragged through a hedge, and had so little meat on him that a gust of wind would blow him away. Joe exclaimed, "He'll be captain of this club one day!" The youngster was Mike Milligan.

GROUNDS FOR MOVING

From 1895 a team from Oldham played their first football fixtures at Berry's Field, which was at the rear of the Garforth Methodist Church on Garforth Street, Chadderton. In 1897 they formed a new club and adopted the name of Pine Villa as they rented Hudson Fold at the Pine Mill. They then moved to the Shiloh ground in 1898. This ground was situated on a plot of land behind the Rifle Range pub on land now occupied by the Elk Mill industrial estate. In 1899 they took over the athletic grounds which coincided with a change of name to Oldham Athletic. The athletic grounds later became known as Boundary Park. In the 1900/01 season there was a dispute over rent and Athletic moved back to Hudson Fold, a pitch near Westhulme Hospital where they stayed until 1906. Their final move was back to Boundary Park on Sheepfoot Lane where they have remained ever since.

FRIENDLY GAME PART OF THE DEAL

Mark Ward signed from non-league side Northwich Victoria for a fee of £10,000 in July 1983. The transfer included a clause that a friendly game be played at Victoria's Drill Field ground on the 9th August in the same year. The game resulted in a 1-1 draw with Tony Henry scoring for the Latics and Northwich retained all the proceeds as agreed. Ward went on to appear in all 46 league and cup matches in the 1983/84 season and he also attained a 100 per cent appearance record in the following season. His consistent midfield displays convinced West Ham United to shell out £250,000 for his services in August 1985.

DENIS IRWIN

Denis Irwin signed for Athletic on a free transfer from Leeds United in May 1986 and went on to establish himself as one of the best full-backs outside the First Division. He made his Latics debut at Derby County in winning style, a Ron Futcher goal being the only marker in the game. Irwin appeared in 204 Oldham games and scored seven goals, most of them rockets from free kicks. He was transferred to Manchester United in June 1990, for £625,000, Athletic's record incoming fee, after giving consistently good service and missing very few games. Athletic also received another £75,000 when Irwin played against Wales at Wrexham in 1991 as a 'three full international games' clause was brought into effect. He went on to give 12 years' excellent service to United and was then given a free transfer to Wolverhampton Wanderers where he ended his playing career. Denis also appeared 56 times for the Republic of Ireland and scored four international goals.

SHANKS SCORES AGAINST LATICS

During the Second World War, many clubs played in regional league competitions and were allowed to use guest players. The players were usually servicemen in the Armed Forces who were stationed nearby. Bill Shankly, the future legendary Liverpool manager, was transferred with his unit to Scotland and played for East Fife. However, the following season he played in two games for Bolton Wanderers while he was on leave and scored one of their goals in a 3-0 victory over Athletic.

SECOND DIVISION CHAMPIONS

Athletic began the 1990/91 season like most teams did – praying and hoping for success on the field. They had dragged themselves out of the doldrums to become firmly established as a respected Second Division force. The new season opened with a very useful 3-2 away win at Wolverhampton Wanderers, where Ian Marshall justified Joe Royle's decision of a switch from defence to attack by hitting a hat-trick to reply to England international Steve Bull's brace. The first home game saw a visit from Leicester City when Marshall scored again and Andy Ritchie also added a goal which gave the home side a 2-0 win. The next three games over Portsmouth, Barnsley and Oxford United were also victorious and left the Latics as league leaders and three points ahead of Sheffield Wednesday. The five wins equalled their best-ever start to a season, a record which went back to 1930. The win over Notts County broke the Latics record of 13 games undefeated in a start to a season that went back to 1953. In November, when Athletic demolished Watford 4-0 at home, they set a new club record of going 16 league games without defeat at the start of a season and the win put them four points ahead of second-placed West Ham United. Their first defeat came in a 1-0 loss at Port Vale on November 17th. The best win of the season came when they hammered Brighton & Hove Albion 6-1 in a game watched by 11,426. Wolves were then demolished 4-1, thus completing the double over the Black Country team. A 2-0 success over Barnsley recorded another double for the season. As February began, the boys succumbed to their heaviest defeat of the season when they crumbled to a 5-1 reverse at Oxford United, Neil Adams scoring the consolation goal. The result left Athletic five points behind leaders West Ham, but with a game in hand. Ritchie scored two goals over his previous employers at Brighton, his second one being hailed as the Goal of the Season. When Palmer scored in the 2-2 tie at Swindon Town he reached a personal milestone as it was his 150th league and cup goal for the club. Another 2-1 success over West Bromwich Albion was followed by a disastrous 2-1 home defeat by relegation-haunted Hull City, their first home loss in over a year. It became a nervous time for followers of the Latics, especially when they lost 2-0 in their next game at struggling Blackburn. Were the wheels falling off again in a season that had promised so much? The next game would be a big test as the visitors were the joint leaders from Upton Park. In the Good Friday game watched by just short of 17,000 excited supporters, it took a late Ritchie penalty to snatch a point after the Hammers keeper Ludek Miklosko had played out of his skin. When the team eked out a 2-1 success over Bristol City it left Joe Royle's boys needing just a point to practically guarantee automatic promotion. With the winning post in sight, the team went to Ipswich and an estimated 3,000 Oldham fans among the 12,000 plus gate were not to be disappointed as two goals from poacher supreme Marshall secured a 2-1 win to send the visiting fans into raptures. The job was done: now to see if they could add the cream and win the championship. The final match of the season against Sheffield Wednesday has been well-documented *(qv)* and the scenes at the end of an amazing season will be remembered forever by those fortunate enough to have witnessed the 3-2 win that clinched the championship with virtually the last kick of the season. The final table was as follows:

	P	W	D	L	F	A	W	D	L	F	A	Pts	GD
Oldham Athletic	46	17	5	1	55	21	8	8	7	28	32	88	+30
West Ham United	46	15	6	2	41	18	9	9	5	19	16	87	+26
Sheffield Weds	46	12	10	1	43	23	10	6	7	37	28	82	+29
Notts County	46	14	4	5	45	28	9	7	7	31	27	80	+21
Millwall	46	11	6	6	43	28	9	7	7	27	23	73	+19
Brighton & HA	46	12	4	7	37	31	9	3	11	26	38	70	-6
Middlesbrough	46	12	4	7	36	17	8	5	10	30	30	69	+19
Barnsley	46	13	7	3	39	16	6	5	12	24	32	69	+15
Bristol City	46	14	5	4	44	28	6	2	15	24	43	67	-3
Oxford United	46	10	9	4	41	29	4	10	9	28	37	61	+3
Newcastle United	46	8	10	5	24	22	6	7	10	25	34	59	-7
Wolverhampton W	46	11	6	6	45	35	2	13	8	18	28	58	0
Bristol Rovers	46	11	7	5	29	20	4	6	13	27	39	58	-3
Ipswich Town	46	9	8	6	32	28	4	10	9	28	40	57	-8
Port Vale	46	10	4	9	32	24	5	8	10	24	40	57	-8
Charlton Athletic	46	8	7	8	27	25	5	10	8	30	36	56	-4
Portsmouth	46	10	6	7	34	27	4	5	14	24	43	53	-12
Plymouth Argyle	46	10	10	3	36	20	2	7	14	18	48	53	-14
Blackburn Rovers	46	8	6	9	26	27	6	4	13	25	39	52	-15
Watford	46	5	8	10	24	32	7	7	9	21	27	51	-14
Swindon Town	46	8	6	9	31	30	4	8	11	34	43	50	-8
Leicester City	46	12	4	7	41	33	2	4	17	19	50	50	-23
West Brom Alb	46	7	11	5	26	21	3	7	13	26	40	48	-9
Hull City	46	6	10	7	35	32	4	5	14	22	53	45	-28

OLDHAM ATHLETIC MANAGERS

David Ashworth	April 1906 to April 1914
	January 1923 to July 1924
Herbert Bamlett	June 1914 to May 1921
Charlie Roberts	July 1921 to December 1922
Bob Mellor	July 1924 to July 1927
	July 1932 to May 1933
	May 1934 to February 1945
Andrew Wilson	July 1927 to July 1932
Jimmy McMullan	May 1933 to May 1934
Frank Womack	February 1945 to April 1947
Billy Wootton	June 1947 to September 1950
George Hardwick	November 1950 to May 1956
Ted Goodier	May 1956 to June 1958
Norman Dodgin	July 1958 to May 1960
Danny McLennan	May to June 1960
Jack Rowley	July 1960 to May 1963
	October 1968 to December 1969
Les McDowell	June 1963 to March 1965
Gordon Hurst	May 1965 to January 1966
Jimmy McIlroy	January 1966 to August 1968
Jimmy Frizzell	March 1970 to June 1982
Joe Royle	June 1982 to November 1994
	March 2009 to May 2009
Graeme Sharp	November 1994 to February 1997
Neil Warnock	February 1997 to May 1998
Andy Ritchie	May 1998 to October 2001
John Sheridan/Bill Urmson	October 2001 to November 2001
Mick Wadsworth	November 2001 to May 2002
Iain Dowie	May 2002 to December 2003
John Sheridan/David Eyres	December 2003 to March 2004
Brian Talbot	March 2004 to February 2005
Tony Philliskirk	February 2005 to March 2005
Ronnie Moore	March 2005 to June 2006
John Sheridan	June 2006 to March 2009
Dave Penney	May 2009 onwards

CHRIS MOORE

In 2001, Oxford-based businessman Chris Moore purchased Oldham Athletic promising that they would return to Premier League football within five years. With Iain Dowie in charge of the team, and after spending heavily, the Latics made it to the Division Two play-offs in the 2002/03 season but they eventually lost out against Queens Park Rangers. Much to the anger of fans, Moore decided to end his interest with the club, leaving behind large debts and a weak squad. He then systematically went about selling the better players at a fraction of their market value to raise as much cash as possible. Oldham were in deep financial trouble and funds were so hard for the club that Dowie, along with the remaining members of the squad, was not paid for several months. The manager tried to stick out the post for as long as possible until he decided to move on citing the need to support his family as a reason. He left Oldham and went to manage Crystal Palace.

MONEY RAISING

In 1981 Athletic discussed the possibility of introducing an OAFC premium bond to help raise money for the club. An ambitious syndicate of ten local companies offered the club £40,000 to win the 1982/83 FA Cup but the club went out at the first hurdle on January 8th in a third round tie at home to Fulham which they lost 2-0. Other money raising schemes at the club have included the Moonraker lottery, Starline, 200 Club and the Mini-Metro lottery.

FIRST SPONSORS

Umbro International Ltd were accepted to provide the new kit for the 1976/77 season and the idea of the possibility of players' kit being sponsored for raising money was considered for the first time. In 1980 Umbro offered the club a three-year contract for the rights to supply the Oldham Athletic kit but the deal went to Redsure Ltd. of Oldham who were given the go-ahead to sponsor the shirts in a £3,000 deal. Redsure thereby became the club's first shirt sponsors.

BOBBY JOHNSTONE

Bobby Johnstone, who died in Selkirk on August 22nd 2001 aged 71, will be fondly remembered as Athletic's biggest-ever crowd-puller and best-loved entertainer. He was the master craftsman of his trade – clever on the ball, a supreme footballing artist, a talented exponent of the weighted pass and a player who, with one sway of the hips, would often leave defenders literally going the wrong way. Bernard Halford was assistant secretary in those magical days of the early 1960s and recalled; "He transformed the club, no doubt about that. He had the crowds flocking down Sheepfoot Lane, even though Athletic were in the Fourth Division. I think it was the only period in my life when I regularly told lies. On matchdays the phone never stopped ringing. 'Is Johnstone playing?' Bobby might have been sitting in my office with his ankle in plaster, but I had to say he was playing otherwise the fans wouldn't have turned up. It really was as cut and dried as that." After a memorable career with Hibernian (twice) and Manchester City, with whom he made history in 1955 and 1956 by becoming the first player to score in successive Wembley FA Cup finals, Johnstone was brought to Oldham by Jack Rowley in the autumn of 1960. The club's average crowd was 4,000, but when Johnstone lined up for his debut on October 15th of that memorable year there was an official attendance of 17,116. The Johnstone era was under way. Bobby made a scoring debut in a 5-2 win and immediately earned himself a place in the hearts and minds of Athletic fans, who were crying out for success after many lean years. Nearly 42,000 crammed into Boundary Park in January, 1962 when a Johnstone-inspired Athletic gave mighty Liverpool the fright of their lives before going down 2-1 in the FA Cup. Halford takes up the story; "In the promotion season of 1962/63, we scored 95 league goals and half of them were scored by Bert Lister (30) and Colin Whitaker (17). Most of them were created by Bobby. He missed one penalty in the whole of his career – against Exeter at Boundary Park when the keeper moved early, and he was so accurate that he could pop them in off a post. I recall that when Les McDowall became manager there was a period when he kept Bobby out of the team. It struggled badly without him and in the end the manager was forced to bring him back. Restored to the team, and with a point to prove, he turned on one of the finest exhibitions of individual skill I've ever seen. It was real 'bag of tricks' stuff and the crowd loved it. Athletic won 2-0 and as the teams left the field, one fan went up to Les and shouted, 'Now you know why 10,000 of us were right... and you were wrong!' Eventually, Les brought young Jim Bowie down from Scotland to replace the maestro. Jim was a talented young player who went on to do a good job for Athletic. But, one day Les was heard to ask Bobby what he thought of the youngster. 'He's a good lad,' came the reply... 'but at his age I had been capped eight times by Scotland!' It tended to put things in perspective and that was not being disrespectful to Jim. Few players were on the same plane as Bobby. He was a fantastic player, who provided me and many thousands of Oldham football followers with the sort of memories they will cherish forever." Jimmy Frizzell asked of his fellow Scot; "What on earth would he have been worth in today's football market place? He had great ability, he was a tremendous reader of the game, he had an astute footballing brain and he had superb touch. His best days were at Hibs, but Latics fans will take a lot of convincing." After finishing his football career, Johnstone played cricket for Hollinwood and became an accomplished crown-green bowler who represented Hollinwood Institute and Springbank. What did Bobby achieve as a player? The greatest ever Latics player: without him Oldham Athletic may not have existed today. Latics' biggest-ever crowd puller. Part of the Famous Five – Johnstone, Gordon Smith, Lawrie Reilly, Eddie Turnbull and Willie Ormond who all played in the forward line together, all became Scottish internationals and scored over 100 goals for Hibernian. The first player to score in two consecutive Wembley FA Cup finals. In 1960 Bobby joined Oldham and his debut saw an unbelievable attendance of 17,116 for a Fourth Division match. Bobby played 143 games for the Latics and scored 36 goals. He played 17 times for Scotland and scored 10 times. He won the Scottish league title with Hibernian twice (1951 and 1952), won the FA Cup with Manchester City in 1956, represented the Scottish Football League six times, appeared for the Great Britain team against the rest of Europe. Retired with grace.

A REAL PRE-MATCH WARM UP

Ex club captain Glenn Keeley used to warm up in an unusual fashion, always partaking of a wee tot of whisky in the players' tunnel en route to the field.

DAVE HODKINSON REMINISCES

Dave Hodkinson was on Athletic's books between 1960 and 1964 and recalls, "I was a shy 16-year-old then and didn't talk much, although for what it's worth, I thought Peter Phoenix was a great guy. He was always friendly and we played alongside each other in the reserves for two seasons on and off. He used to think Jack Rowley wasn't too keen on him for some reason. Jimmy Rollo was a real joker. He'd say, 'Let's play a fast game in the second half then I can get home early'. Johnny Bollands used to let some real 'stinkers' go in the dressing room. Brian Jarvis was a quiet but popular guy and he and Jimmy Frizzell were inseparable bachelors in those days. Bob Ledger, great right-winger, was also an amiable fellow and went out of his way to talk to younger players. John McCue and Bill Spurdle – I never got to know too well. It was a sense of them having come to the close of a good career and just playing out the time. I used to think Bert Lister was a great centre-forward. He used to bang them in in training just like he did in a game. And, of course, Bobby Johnstone was the best passer of a ball I've ever seen. Billy Dearden and I palled around a bit. After making my Latics debut I was flavour of the month but it coincided with the England youth trials taking place at the Cliff. I was sent along from Oldham as the token Fourth Division player. The trials consisted of two days of games and I found myself being marked by Len Badger who was to go on to play several hundred games with Sheffield United. I never got past him once! Tommy Smith was on team 'one' given that he was already an 'up and comer' at Liverpool. I daren't go anywhere near him, he was absolutely fearsome; huge thighs, snarling countenance; he didn't need to tackle any other 16-year-olds – just look at them! George Jones who played for Bury about the same time as I played at Oldham was also in the trial and he ended up at Oldham. The Cliff had other memories and in one Oldham 'A' game I played against George Best who was about a year younger than me. I don't remember how he played that day but I recall my dad singing the praises of 'that little, black-haired winger playing for United'."

HORWICH HELP OUT

Horwich RMI allowed the Latics to use their ground for 16 Lancashire League games and 5 trial games for a fee of £400 in 1975.

WELCOME TO THE SECOND DIVISION

Athletic made their league debut in the Second Division at Stoke City on September 9th 1907. The game was billed as a mis-match, due to the fact that the Potters had spent most of their life in the First Division. David Walders was captain on the day and he proudly led his team to a memorable 3-1 victory in front of around 12,000 spectators. The first-ever goal scored for Oldham in the league was hit by Billy Dodds. Watkins levelled for Stoke in the second half but a headed goal from debutant Frank Newton, and another from another debutant Jimmy Swarbrick, completed the scoring.

WOMEN'S FOOTBALL

So women's football is a new thing is it? On May 14th 1921, 698 people turned up to watch a ladies' game at Boundary Park when Chorley Ladies played St. Helen's Ladies. Another game, the FIFA World Cup for Women when England entertained Norway at Boundary Park, was played on May 14th 1998.

UNUSUAL ROYLE VISIT

When Joe Royle arrived at Boundary Park to take up his duties at Boundary Park in June 1982, he arrived on the back of a lorry. His car had broken down on the M62 motorway and he had to hitch a lift to meet the press. He quipped, "My first job as manager will be to get a reliable car."

CONTRACT MYSTERY

When Latics manager Iain Dowie decided to move on from Oldham Athletic he wanted to approach Crystal Palace with a view to taking over the vacant manager's job at the Eagles. As he was under contract, he was refused permission to talk to Palace and it would have been a breach of his contract to do so. Athletic's owners confronted him and Dowie responded; "Show me the contract!" Mysteriously, the contract had completely disappeared and it could not be found anywhere. Subsequently, Dowie went to Palace for the interview and resigned as Athletic manager on December 19th 2003, only to take over at Selhurst Park a couple of days later.

BEST AND WORST RUNS

Longest winning run: 10 .... Jan 12th 1974 to Mar 16th 1974
Longest losing run: 6 .... Feb 5th 2005 to Feb 26th 2005
Longest unbeaten run: 17 .... Aug 25th 1990 to Nov 10th 1990
Longest unbeaten home run: 38 .... Feb 4th 1989 to 24th Mar 1990
Longest run without a win: 17 .... Sep 9th 1920 to Dec 25th 1920
Longest run of away wins: 7 .... Nov 6th 2007 to Jan 5th 2008

THE DURHAM WONDERBOY

Kenny Chaytor, The Durham Wonderboy, was with Athletic from 1954 to 1960, making his debut when he was still only 16-years-old against Gateshead. George Hardwick was the player-manager and he said that Kenny was the only young player he knew that didn't have to be taught anything. He would surely go on to play for England. Well, it didn't quite work out that way but he stayed at Oldham for seven seasons and holds a particular claim to fame that many fans wouldn't know. His three goals against Mansfield Town in January 1955, at the tender age of 17 years and 72 days, made him the youngest player ever to score a league hat-trick in the history of the game. His feat has only been surpassed once since that date; by Trevor Francis in 1971. After scoring 20 times in 77 league appearances, Chaytor left the club, and played for four more seasons with Ashton United and Witton Albion before returning to the north-east. He married an Oldham lass, had three children, two of them born in Oldham, continued life as a toolmaker, temporarily emigrated to Canada and is now happily retired in Trimdon, Co. Durham. He was last seen at Boundary Park for the FA Cup tie with Huddersfield in 2008, his first visit to the ground for over thirty years. It must have brought back some memories…

CAN WE TRADE INSTEAD?

When Newcastle United offered £200,000 cash for John Ryan in June 1983, manager Joe Royle intimated that he would prefer to transfer Ryan, along with Paul Atkinson in exchange for the Magpies' highly-rated Imre Varadi. The exchange idea was not accepted and Varadi never came to Oldham.

GATE RECEIPTS AND TICKET PRICES

Oldham played Manchester City in the First Division on September 1st 1919. The game was a 6.30pm kick-off and it had been raining heavily all day. The 4,587 hardy fans had paid a total of £230 6s 0d of which City took £31 7s 2d. On January 10th 1920, the Latics entertained Cardiff City and the receipts were £1,938 1s 6d, the first time the club had taken in excess of a thousand pounds. Another game on April 30th 1920 was played against Hurst in the Manchester Senior Cup, the takings were £92 13s 4d, of which the referee and linesmen were paid £2 9s 6d, the police received £1 10s 0d and Hurst FC claimed travelling fares of £1 5s 0d. Approximately 20% of all takings used to go as entertainment/amusement tax. As an example, the First Division game at home to Burnley on November 20th 1920 brought in £1,079 4s 0d. Of this, the club's takings were £838 0s 11d and the tax paid was £241 0s 7d. For the 1974/75 season, the season ticket prices were set as follows: VP box £40; VP stand £30; Private box £27.50p; Ford Stand £14; Wing stand £11.50p; Main paddock £9; Ford paddock £9 and the Chaddy End stand was £9. In the main stand it was only 60p on the day, and 40p in the ground. The club introduced a family season ticket for the wings of the Ford Stand priced at £52.50 which would admit one adult and a school child to each league match for the 1980/81 season. A total of 9,500 free tickets were issued to Oldham's secondary schools for the Cambridge United game on the December 11th 1982. Athletic's best gate receipts were £138,680, the day they entertained Manchester United on December 29th 1993 in the Premiership.

NO POINTS DEDUCTION

When Athletic entered administration in October 2003, the only good news to come out of the deal was that they did not get deducted any league points. They entered the unenviable position just before the Football League started to penalise clubs for such indiscretions. The ten-point deduction rule for Football League clubs entering administration was introduced in 2004, with Wrexham being the first league club to suffer a deduction in the 2004/05 season.

FORTRESS BOUNDARY PARK

Between January 1989 and September 1991 – a period of 32 months – Oldham Athletic lost only two league games at home out of a possible 72, including cup ties! Some remarkable wins were achieved during the run: 5-3 over Portsmouth; 4-0 over Ipswich Town; 7-0 over Scarborough; 6-0 over West Ham United; 4-1 over Ipswich Town; 4-1 over Watford; 6-1 over Brighton & Hove Albion; 4-1 over Wolverhampton Wanderers; 5-3 over Plymouth Argyle and 3-0 over Chelsea.

CHAMPAGNE BREAKFAST ANYONE?

When the team played in the second leg of the League Cup semi-final in 1990 they flew down for the game at West Ham. On the return flight, chairman Ian Stott bought everyone champagne and the team ended up in the Black Ladd pub at Grains Bar for a steak and chips dinner/breakfast which finished somewhere around four o'clock in the morning. Rick Holden took the responsibility for driving home a slightly tipsy Denis Irwin in his red Ford Cosworth.

PLAYING AGAINST YOUR HERO

When Dick Mulvaney signed for Oldham Athletic he was in dispute with Blackburn Rovers who has listed him at a £50,000 fee. With no bids coming in the Football League granted him a free transfer and Jimmy Frizzell stepped in to land the popular defender. Dick later admitted that although playing at a higher level with Blackburn Rovers, Oldham was the most enjoyable part of his playing career. Winning the Third Division championship as captain was his best achievement in football. In his earlier days in the north-east every young man wanted nothing more than to play football. One of Dick's heroes was Charlie Hurley and Dick used to watch Charlie play for Sunderland at Roker Park at a time when the club were known as 'The Bank Of England' team of the fifties. They won a few First Division titles, the last of which was in 1936. In later years, when Charlie was at the end of his career, Dick played in a game against him. Dick said, "It was fantastic coming up for a corner and being marked by my boyhood hero." Dick quipped, "I was better than him then."

NORTHERN IRELAND INTERNATIONALS

The following Latics players have represented Northern Ireland at international level but not necessarily while they were playing on Oldham's books.

Billy Dodds 1907-08 .... 2 IL Xl apps
William Andrews 1908-09 .... 3 caps and 6 IL Xl apps
Jimmy Reid 1908-10 .... 4 IL Xl apps
John Mitchell 1909-10 .... 4 IL Xl apps
William Halligan 1920-21 .... 2 caps, 2 victory int'ls and 1 IL Xl app
Lawrie Cumming 1929-30 .... 3 caps
Tommy Davis 1935-38 .... 1 cap
Pat Broadley 1951-53 .... 3 IL Xl apps
Bill Marshall 1962-64 .... U-23
Ally Doyle 1965-69 .... schoolboy and youth
Mike Nolan 1966-68 .... schoolboy
Billy Johnston 1966-68 .... 2 caps and 7 IL Xl apps
Jimmy McIlroy 1966-68 .... 55 caps, 2 IL Xl apps and 1 GB app
Ray Smith 1966-69 .... schoolboy
Ronnie Blair 1966-69 & 1972-80 .... 5 caps
Allan Hunter 1967-69 .... amateur, U-23 and 53 caps
Eric McGee 1967-69 .... youth, amateur and 2 IL Xl apps
Aaron Callaghan 1986-88 .... U-21, U-17 and youth
Alan McNeill 1969-75 .... amateur
Derek Spence 1970-73 .... youth and 29 caps
Norman Kelly 1987-90 .... U-16, schoolboys and U-21
David Miskelly 1996-2003 .... youth and U-21
Ben Burgess 2003 .... U-21
Mark Hughes 2004-06 .... every level and 2 caps
Alan Blaney 2007 .... U-19, U-21 and 5 caps
John Thompson 2006-09 .... 3 caps
Shane Supple 2009 .... U-21

SILVERWARE AGAIN

When Athletic beat Barrow 2-0 on May 9th 1967 they walked away with the Lancashire Senior Cup trophy for the first time in 59 years.

LATICS AND THE JAPS ATTACK ON THE SAME DAY...

In the game on December 6th 1941, the half-time announcement was that the Japanese had attacked Pearl Harbor. It was wartime and the third season of wartime football as the Latics disposed of Halifax Town 6-2.

FA CUP SEMI-FINAL 1993/94

Oldham reached the FA Cup semi-final for the second time in four seasons and once again had to face their old adversaries, Manchester United. The match was played at Wembley Stadium on April 10th 1994 in front of 56,399 fans, but unlike the previous exciting, end-to-end, goal cluttered semi-final game between the two teams, this match was a dour affair. The early excitement was centred around a penalty appeal after Neil Pointon was pushed off the ball in the third minute by Lee Sharpe, an incident which the TV cameras proved to be a valid penalty claim. The best that United could muster was a header by Paul Ince but the Latics set up a flowing move in the 26th minute through Pointon, Darren Beckford and Rick Holden, but Graeme Sharp fluffed the chance by shooting wide. Early in the second half Peter Schmeichel had to be alert after Sharp sent him scampering low to keep out his effort. True to form, the game went into extra time. Pointon sent the Oldham fans into ecstasy when he fired Athletic into the lead in the 106th minute of the game. It was his first goal of the season and it all looked to be going Oldham's way as they were holding on to their slender 1-0 advantage until Mark Hughes broke the hearts of the Latics by scoring a last-gasp levelling goal with a superb volley in the last minute of extra time. Athletic were literally seconds away from one of their finest moments in their 99-year history but their hopes were left shattered and they would have to go through it all again.

PA SYSTEM

A new PA system was purchased in 1979, which cost a total of £300. It was a disco deck type system, which was recommended by Piccadilly Radio to improve the quality of the pre- and mid-match entertainment.

FA CUP SEMI-FINAL: OLDHAM V MANCHESTER UNITED AT WEMBLEY ON APRIL 10TH 1994

THE PORT VALE FLYER

4-4-2, 4-3-3, 5-3-1 – or 52248? Not a number to readily slip off the tongues of Latics statisticians, but it was to become infamous with supporters. 52248 was the number of a former 'Lanky' class steam engine that regularly shunted in the Oldham Mumps area as one of the resident goods pilots. On December 2nd 1952, 52248 was minding its own business and was called upon to haul a Latics supporters' special to Port Vale for the second round FA Cup tie. The engine scheduled for the job had failed near Rochdale, and the Mumps Station master was informed that the train would be heavily delayed. The large throng of supporters became restless and some were becoming menacing so the master requested another engine from control to be told there was nothing available. With the crowd growing quite ugly, he took it upon himself to commandeer the pilot and put it in charge of a scratch set of coaching stock from Mumps siding. The engine was facing the wrong way and the Lees footplate crew were reluctant, but were convinced to take the fans to Stockport where they were told that they would be relieved. The 0-6-0 was in a run down state, hence its menial duties at Mumps, but it did eventually get away, much to the relief of the station master. Upon reaching Stockport Edgeley the Lees crew were informed that there was not another engine available and the Stockport crew refused to take the engine south as they thought it was only fit for the scrap heap. The Lees men unfortunately didn't know the road! After much negotiating, and with constant barracking from the restless Oldham fans, the Stockport men agreed to continue the journey. All went well until a hot axle-box on the tender failed near their destination and a relief engine from Stoke shed was sent to the rescue. The supporters arrived at Port Vale just in time to see the last 20 minutes of the game that the Latics won 3-0 with goals from Eric Gemmell (2) and Bill Ormond. The gate was officially recorded at 25,398 and one wonders if the Latics fans were accounted for as the gates used to open at three-quarter time in those days. The 52248 returned to Lees shed some days later and was unofficially christened 'THE PORT VALE FLYER'. The poor station master became very unpopular and local tradition has it that questions were later asked in the House of Commons.

IF YOU WANT ME, PAY ME

When Keith Hicks, left Athletic he did so because of money. He admitted that the club were prepared to offer better incentives for incoming players than they would for their home-grown talent. Although Hicks took a drop in playing standard of two divisions when he joined Hereford United in 1980, the man with the chin earned a signing-on fee in addition to an extra £50 in wages per week.

TEXACO CUP

Athletic have taken part in the Texaco Cup (1974/75) and Anglo-Scottish Cup (1977/78 and 1980/81) on three occasions. Keith Hicks and John Hurst top the appearance charts in the competition with 17 outings each. Ronnie Blair appeared 16 times.

FOUR PLAYERS HIT DOUBLE FIGURES

When Athletic won the Second Division championship in 1991 they finished the season as the top home goalscorers in the Second Division with a total of 55 goals. They were also the top overall scorers in the division with 88. They could not be matched by many teams as they also boasted four players that had hit double figures for the year: Ian Marshall (18); Neil Redfearn (17); Andy Ritchie (15) and Roger Palmer (10).

LEAVE ME ALONE

It's strange the type of rigmaroles some players go through before games. When goalkeeper Les Pogliacomi used to travel away on the team bus he would never talk to anyone. He would merely sit alone and listen to his music or watch a DVD until he arrived at his destination.

ANDY'S FAREWELL

Legend Andy Ritchie made his last senior appearance for Oldham Athletic as a late substitute on January 9th 2001 in a home Associate Members Cup tie against Wigan Athletic. Wigan won the game 3-2; Latics' goals were scored by Phil Salt and Matty Tipton. Ritchie was 41 at the time.

PROGRAMMES

A matchday programme is part and parcel of many football fans' experiences but it can be quite an expensive part of the day out. Just after the war the cost of an Oldham Athletic programme was 2d and it stayed that way until the price was increased by a penny for the 1952/53 season. The threepenny programme lasted until the 1961/62 season when it suddenly doubled in price to 6d. When Ken Bates took over Athletic in 1966 he introduced the new *Boundary Bulletin* which was an extravagant but revolutionary publication which was well worth the increased cost of 1/-. When Bates left the club the Bulletin ceased and for the 1968/69 term the cost of a matchday read was reduced to 9d. Programme costs were raised to 7p when decimalisation appeared in 1972 and remained that way until 1974/75 when the new *Boundary News* jumped up in price to 10p. An increase of 2p to 12p might have been hard to swallow in 1977/78 but the following year the *Athletic Review* shot up to a massive 20p. Into the 1980s and footballing expenses were still rising so it was decided to charge 30p – but from 1981-2 it cost 35p. It rose yet again to 40p for 1983/84 and then shot up to 50p between 1984 and 1987. Another 10p was added the following term and the 1980s were seen out by fans paying 80p for a programme. Prices spiralled in the 1990s when the first £1 programme, the *Oldham Athletic Gazette*, was introduced and it rose to £1.20p from 1992-94 with another 10p being added the following season. From 1995 to 1998 the going rate was £1.50 but the cost was £1.80p as the club entered the new millennium. The first £2 matchday programme appeared from 2000-02 when it increased to £2.50p and that's how it stayed until 2007. Today, you will need to part with £3 for a copy of the *Latics Blue Pride*, the official matchday magazine.

PLEASEA PASTA CHICKEN

When Canadian international Carlo Corazzin was playing for Athletic he always had to have the same meal the night before games. This consisted of chicken breast with pasta and salad. On game days, the morning always began with poached eggs on toast with baked beans. He never deviated from this superstition.

INTERNATIONAL PLAYERS

The following Latics have represented their countries at international level but not necessarily while they were on Oldham's books.

Stan Ackerley (Australia)	1961-62	28 caps
Winston Dubose (USA)	1988-92	14 caps
Gunnar Halle (Norway)	1991-96	64 caps
Junior Agogo (Ghana)	1999	21 caps
J. P. Kalala (DR Congo)	2007-08	6 caps
Carl Valentine (Canada)	1976-80	31 caps
Tore Andre Pedersen (Norway)	1993-94	46 caps
Toddy Orlygsson (Iceland)	1995-97	41 caps
Bruce Grobbelaar (Zimbabwe)	1997-98	33 caps
Cristian Colusso (Argentina)	2002	U-20 and U-23
Mark Watson (Canada)	2000	77 caps
Carlo Corazzin (Canada)	2000-03	59 caps
Louis Lourenco Da Silva (Portugal)	2002	U-16 to U-21
Chris Killen (New Zealand)	2002-06	U-23 and 26 caps
Kangaga Ndiwa-Lord (DR Congo)	2003	1 cap
Jermain Johnson (Jamaica)	2003-04	40 caps
Neil Kilkenny (Australia)	2004-05, 2007	U-23 and 2 caps
Stefan Stam (Holland)	2004-07	U-18 and U-20
Rodney Jack (St. Vincent)	2004-05	75 caps
Tomasz Cywka (Poland)	2006	U-21
Darren Byfield (Jamaica)	2008-09	6 caps

DRAWN AGAIN

Andy Ritchie had an unusual habit before a game. He would take a bath before kick-off and team-mates would joke that he was a "smelly person".

HIGH SCORERS

In four consecutive home games between November and December 1990 the team scored 19 goals. The 4-1, 6-1, 4-1 and 5-3 victories came, respectively, over Watford, Brighton & Hove Albion, Wolverhampton Wanderers and Plymouth Argyle.

UNUSUAL MIDDLE NAMES

Finlay 'Ballantine' Speedie 1908-09

Thomas 'Higginson' Broad 1909-11

Alexander 'Leck' 'Brown' Downie 1909-11

Alfred 'Vickers' Toward 1909-13

Samuel 'Turnell' Pilkington 1911-12

Edward 'Hallows' Taylor 1912-22

Richard 'Wright' Carlisle 1919-21

John 'Gaiger' Nord 1919-22

Alexander 'Ferguson' Campbell 1920-22

Reginald 'Fidelas' Vincent Freeman 1921-23

George 'Boyd' Waddell 1922

David 'McLachlan' Spence 1922-23

Archibald 'McDonald' Longmuir 1923-24

Roger 'Cowburn' Seddon 1925-26

John 'Arden' 'Brown' Maddison 1927-29

Lawrence Stanley 'Slater' Cumming 1929-30

Austin 'Wilkinson' Trippier 1931-32

Henry 'Bowater' Rowley 1933-34

John 'Pattison' Richardson 1935-36

Robert 'Curry' Talbot 1935-36

Henry 'Boyce' Church 1935-37

John 'Theodore' 'Knight' Clarke 1935-37

Herbert 'Kitchener' Blackshaw 1936-38

Thomas Eric 'Rollerson' Shipman 1938-46

Harold 'Kynaston' Tilling 1942-48

Oliver 'Houston' Burns 1946-47

John 'Hilary' Fryer 1947-48

Francis 'Adamson' McCormack 1949-53

James 'Ferguson' Munro 1950-53

George Francis 'Moutry' Hardwick 1950-56

John 'Campbell' Crawford 1952-54

George 'Syme' Torrance 1956-57

John Theodore 'Hever' Ferguson 1956-58

Edward 'Cullinane' Murphy 1956-59

Walter 'Bingley' Taylor 1958-60

James Cameron 'Mars' Ferguson 1959-60

Alexander 'Halley' Wann 1960-61
James 'Shepherd' Rollo 1960-63
James 'Letson' Frizzell 1960-70
Ian 'Denzil' Greaves 1961-63
Alan Thomas 'Anderson' Swinburne 1961-64
William 'Bell' McGinn 1963-66
Robert 'McAllister' Craig 1964-65
William Robert 'Crawford' Aitken 1966-69
Alan 'Nicholson' Spence 1968-69
Arthur 'Campbell' Thompson 1969-70
Andrew 'Lorimar' Lochhead 1973-74
Gordon 'Duffield' Smith 1986
Earl 'Delisser' Barratt 1987-91
Darren Richard 'Lorenzo' Beckford 1992-95
Orpheo 'Henk' Keizerweerd 1993
Douglas John 'Houston' Hodgson 1997-98
Manuel 'Junior' Agogo 1999
Wayne Michael 'Hill' Andrews 2002-03
Giancarlo 'Michele' Corazzin 2002-03
Rodney 'Alphonso' Jack 2004-05
Anthony Paul Shaun Andrew 'Daure' Grant 2006
Leon 'Marvin' Clarke 2007
Michael 'Barrington' Ricketts 2007
Miguel 'Farrero' Roque 2007
Jason 'Lee Mee' Jarrett 2008

JIMMY FRIZZELL'S TESTIMONIAL

After Jimmy Frizzell was fired as manager in 1982, he was rewarded for his services to the club with a testimonial game and Athletic invited a select Manchester United XI to participate in his honour. The team was made up from United, Manchester City and Liverpool players and Bruce Grobbelaar played in goal for the opposition whereas Frank Worthington guested for the Latics. The wind played a big part in the game, which Athletic eventually won 3-2 – much to the delight of the unusually high number of Oldham fans who had turned out for the occasion. The gate brought in approximately 2,000 extra supporters compared with a regular league game – testament to Frizzell's popularity.

BILLY URMSON, BY REBECCA

"Billy Urmson was a man of many personalities. I am still trying to get to know him. My sister Emma and I were adopted at a young age by Mr & Mrs Urmson and little did we realise what a difference our lives would become. I remember Christmas morning, my sister and I would just be getting up to open our presents and he would be off out the door, because there was something important he had to do because of Oldham Athletic. I remember holidays abroad and long car journeys. He used to keep us interested by giving us players initials and we had to work out the players' names. I got pretty good. My dad loved Oldham, when he woke up in the morning the first thing on his mind was football, I don't just mean football, I mean Oldham Athletic. I can't describe his love, I really wish I could. His love for Oldham came before his family. He loved his family but the love he felt for Oldham Athletic is indescribable. It was like an obsession. He tried so hard; he gave his all and more. When I was young I was jealous of Oldham Athletic, for the simple reason my dad wasn't there on my birthday or Christmas, Oldham Athletic had his love, but as the years went by I found myself loving Oldham the way he did, I felt the same obsession, the same addiction. I came to the point where I looked upon Oldham Athletic and its staff as my family! Then not so long ago [February 2003] the news came that he was being made redundant. It came as a shock to all the family. My dad stayed strong! Then a few weeks later a tumour was found on his lung! The biggest thing that hurt my dad wasn't the tumour, it was the fact that Oldham Athletic was no longer in his life. He felt they had turned their back on him after 27 years. When he had to leave Boundary Park Billy said, "It has been a pleasure to work with Joe and Willie over the last eleven years. Joe is by far the best manager I've ever worked with! Finally, I would like to settle many arguments. I am continually being asked about Joe's best buy over the years… and in my opinion there is no doubt… it has to be the fridge that was in Joe's office where we kept all the Budweisers!"

REDS

Before the formation of Oldham Athletic AFC, the team were playing under the title of Pine Villa and had much success. At that particular time the club colours were not today's blues, but red and white.

LOWEST HOME GATES

The 8-1 preliminary-round FA Cup win over Darwen on December 7th 1907 was watched by approximately 4,000 people, Athletic's lowest-ever recorded FA Cup gate at the time. When wartime came it had a devastating effect on the number of supporters who were able to witness the games. In one such fixture on November 11th 1916, approximately 300 fans bothered to show up for the 4-1 home loss to Rochdale. Another wartime casualty on January 9th 1918 witnessed around 500 soccer-starved supporters see their team lose 4-0 to another local side, Bury. The 5-2 home loss against Blackburn Rovers on May 28th 1940 was watched by an all-time low of just 412 supporters. The support was not much better on December 6th 1941 when the Latics entertained Halifax Town. They won the match 6-2 in front of just 479 people. Hull City came to town for a Third Division (North) game on February 23rd 1957 which was watched by just 2,500 spectators, their lowest at this level. Lewis Brook got the only goal in a 3-1 reverse. On April 12th 1960, only 2,264 supporters came to see the Fourth Division game against Walsall. It could have been a blessing as the Latics crashed 4-2 with Bill Spurdle scoring a rare goal. The other scorer was Brian Birch from the penalty spot. The lowest Third Division gate was recorded as 2,073 when Northampton Town visited Boundary Park on April 29th 1969. Derek Spence scored the only Athletic goal in a 1-1 draw. The League Cup game against Grimsby Town which occurred on August 20th 1996 attracted just 2,975, which was an all-time low for the competition. Orient came to Boundary Park on January 3rd 1986 for a cup tie which was watched by 3,604, Oldham's lowest-ever gate for an FA Cup game. On May 3rd 1986, the home game against Fulham was viewed by 2,510 supporters, the worst attendance since Athletic were promoted back to the Second Division. Tony Henry and Ron Futcher got the goals in a 2-1 win.

LATICS' ENGLAND COACH

Bill Taylor was released from services at Boundary Park to perform his duties as England coach for the game against Eire on February 6th 1980, but only on the condition that he took charge of the Oldham Athletic first team on his return.

'PINCH ME' SEASON STATISTICS

In the 1989/90 season the team played a total of 65 games. It was inevitable that they would run out of steam. Athletic had replaced training sessions with matches as the fixtures came hard and fast. The backlog of games eventually caught up and the players were forced to turn out in nine matches during the month of March. The season was winding down for most teams but for the Latics it was business as usual in April, and that meant another round of tiring games against stiff opponents. When the emotional journey was finally over, Earl Barrett was the only player to have appeared in every game, closely followed by Rick Holden on 64 appearances. Roger Palmer was the leading marksman for the year with 16 goals, which brought his total to 129 all-time goals. The Latics had averaged crowds of 11,240, a huge increase, and their best attendances for ten years. In 33 home games, they had been watched by over a third-of-a-million spectators, so the season had been a success, and was probably their best ever. For the fans that rode the rollercoaster, it will never be forgotten and the foundations were laid for the final push needed to take Oldham Athletic back to the First Division.

ROGER AND OUT!

Roger Palmer bowed out of Athletic in true style. He finally brought down the curtain on his illustrious Athletic career in a Latics reserves game against Scunthorpe at Boundary Park on May 10th 1993. The reserves won 4-2 and 33-year-old Palmer notched two goals; one was his trademark near-post header, scored from a Mark Brennan centre. His other was a spectacular drive from the edge of the box. The reserves were looking for promotion to the Pontins League First Divison and the result left them just 90 minutes away from the top flight. They put out a very strong side for the match: Hallworth, Makin, Barlow, Marshall, Hall, McDonald, Graham, Brennan, Tolson, Palmer and Keizerweerd. Eyre replaced Tolson and Price was an unused sub.

CENTRE OF EXCELLENCE

Athletic's now famous Centre of Excellence was first suggested for the 1984/85 season.

AWAY GAME PLAYED AT HOME

Athletic's fixture at Ewood Park on Boxing Day 1981 was switched to Boundary Park. With Blackburn Rovers' ground frozen and no chance of the game going ahead, the two clubs created a piece of footballing history. It was the first time that a league game had ever been switched although many cup ties had been previously switched. The home advantage did nothing to help the Latics though as they lost the game 3-0. A gate of 15,400 produced record receipts of £24,000.

SHORTEST PLAYING CAREER ON RECORD

When Danny Walsh replaced Mark Innes in the 86th minute of the home game against Burnley on 10th April 1999 it was to be his only appearance for Athletic, and therefore the shortest playing career on record. The game resulted in a 1-1 draw with Matty Tipton scoring the Latics goal in the 37th minute. Andy Payton got the leveller for the Clarets in the 52nd minute in a game watched by 8,542 fans.

THE LONG AND SHORT OF IT

The Latics have had their fair share of tall and short players. Back in the 1960s big Jim Bowie was signed as a replacement for wee Bobby Johnstone and he measured in at 6ft 3ins. A star player from the 1980s was Andy Linighan, who stood 6ft 1ins. One of the tallest players ever to represent the Latics was Ian Ormondroyd. Nicknamed 'The Stick' by the Oldham faithful, Ormondroyd was 6ft 4ins. When Jan Budtz came on loan to Athletic from Hartlepool United in 2009 he succeeded Ormondroyd by one inch, standing 6ft 5ins. Of the smaller players, Bobby McIlvenny, a member of Athletic's 1952/53 championship-winning side, was just under 5ft 4ins. and 10st; the hard working inside-forward was one of the club's smallest players. The crown for the smallest recorded player goes to another 1960s player, Billy Aitken who was a mere 5ft 2ins. without his boots!

NEW BADGE

A new club badge, designed by Stewart Beckett, was approved for introduction in the 1983/84 season.

TEAM ANTHEM

'Mouldy Old Dough' by Lieutenant Pigeon was Athletic's long-time theme tune but rule changes by the Performing Rights Society in March 2009 meant that the song would be heard no more at Boundary Park. The song has been associated with the team for around 30 years and it still brings a tear to the eye of many a supporter as the team run out onto the field to the muffled strains of the all-time Oldham cult tune. The PRS increased their royalty fees by a staggering 600% which meant that Athletic would have needed to shell out £3,900 per year, as opposed to the £700 that existed for the rights to play the song. The society argued that the entrance music – which is played when the teams come out on to the pitch – and goal celebration music are an integral part of matchday entertainment. They classify it differently to general background music. If the club were to simply pay for that, the figure would have reverted to £700 per year, which they would have been happy to pay. At a time when all clubs were looking at ways to save money, they could not justify paying that amount and another piece of history was lost. Maybe when the Latics once again grace the Premiership, and the credit crunch is finally over, they may justify bringing the anthem back from the grave.

GROUND STATISTICS

Ground improvements to Boundary Park in November 1974 increased the capacity by 3,342 to 29,842. After terracing and barrier work at the Rochdale Road end in 1980, the capacity of the ground had been reduced to 24,000; Chadderton Road end 6,100, Rochdale Road end 8,557, Main Stand and Ford Stand paddocks, 3,000 each, with 3,343 seats. With the Broadway Stand now demolished due to future proposed developments, the three-sided ground now housed 3,754 supporters in the Chadderton Road end, with 2,455 fans accommodated in the Main Stand. The Rochdale Road Stand now holds 4,609, which brings the total seating accommodation to 10,818, although the official total stated by the club is 10,638.

BENEFIT GAME

Oldham Athletic played a benefit game in May 1961 in aid of the Players' Benevolent Fund.

OLDEST DEBUTANTS

Jack Warner became the club's oldest debutant at the age of 40 years – minus a week. His debut came at Southport in a 0-0 draw on August 18th 1951. When footballing nomad Bobby Collins joined Athletic near the end of his incredible career he beat Warner when he turned out for Athletic against Wrexham in a 2-2 draw on October 14th 1972, aged 41. His last appearance for the Latics came in his 43rd year on April 20th 1973, in a 0-0 draw at home to Rochdale.

ALAN HARDY

Alan Hardy, formerly commercial manager with Mossley FC, was appointed promotions manager of Oldham Athletic on April 22nd 1981. His remit was to run the new Athletic lottery and he became the commercial manager in October of the same year after the departure of Mike Twiss. Hardy was responsible for obtaining a bank loan of £40,000 to finance the building of a single-storey shop named the 'Latique' in 1988 that was opened for the start of the 1989/90 season. The income generated from the Wembley appearance in the League Cup final in 1990 enabled the club to repay the loan in full and build a second storey to house the club's commercial offices. Mr. Hardy was instrumental in obtaining sponsorship deals that included Bovis, Martins, Maxwell, JD Sports, Slumberland, Carlotti, Carbrini, Pentagon Vauxhall, Detect All Alarms, Seton, George Hill, and Leesfield Developments, and was appointed chief executive in 1997. In his new role, Alan received a prestigious long-service award from the Football League in 2004. He also served on various Football League working parties including the Football League Trophy, Club Criteria, Diversity Advocacy Group and has also served on the management committee for the Central League. Hardy has been a Manchester FA council member since 2002 and is now recognised as one of the longest-serving officials in professional football.

LODGING OUT

Steve Edward's landlady decided that she could not afford to keep him lodging on the £8 a week paid by the club back in January 1975. She requested a raise to £16 a week, but the club offered £15, which was the maximum allowed by Football League rules.

THAT'S JUST BEING GREEDY

For a player to score a hat-trick is a remarkable achievement but anything more than that is just being plain greedy. The following players have gone on to score more than three goals in one game. If the surname only is given, the Christian name is unknown.

Pepper 4	8-0 v Tonge, ML	7th Feb 1903
McDermott 6	13-1 v Parkfield Central, MJC	30th Jan 1904
Plumpton 5	11-0 v Newton-le-Willows, LCB	7th Jan 1905
Shoreman 6	11-0 v Newton-le-Willows, LCB	7th Jan 1905
Elliot Pilkington 4	5-3 v Bolton Wanderers, LSPT	15th Dec 1917
Arthur Gee 4	6-0 v Port Vale, LSPT	22nd Feb 1919
Arthur Ormston 5	7-2 v Stoke City, D2	14th Sep 1925
Bert Watson 4	6-4 v Stockton, FAC	12th Dec 1925
Albert Pynegar 4	8-3 v Nottingham Forest, D2	1st May 1926
Maurice Wellock 4	5-2 v Grimsby Town, D2	12th Feb 1927
'Taffy' Jones 4 (1p)	5-2 v Wrexham, D3(N)	18th Jan 1936
Bert Blackshaw 4	5-1 v Halifax Town, D3(N)	1st May 1948
Eric Gemmell 7	11-2 v Chester, D3(N)	19th Jan 1952
Don Travis 4	5-0 v Bradford City, D3(N)	18th Apr 1955
Bert Lister 6	11-0 v Southport, D3	26th Dec 1962
Ian Towers 4	4-0 v Colchester United, D3	4th Feb 1967
Jimmy Fryatt 4 (1p)	5-0 v Chester, D4	28th Mar 1970
David Shaw 4	5-1 v Brentford, D4	5th Sep 1970
Frankie Bunn 6	7-0 v Scarborough, LC	25th Oct 1989
Graeme Sharp 4	5-1 v Luton Town, D1	11th Apr 1992
Andy Ritchie 4	7-1 v Torquay, LC	24th Sep 1991
Carlo Corazzin 4	5-1 v Wrexham, D2	10th Feb 2001
Clyde Wijnhard 4	6-1 Mansfield Town, D2	14th Sep 2002

HEADS UP

When Athletic beat Gateshead at Boundary Park on February 21st 1948, they won by a convincing 5-3 scoreline. What was unusual about the game was that all five goals were headers. Bill Blackshaw (2), Bill Jessop (2) and Ken Brierley were the marksmen who used their heads on the day.

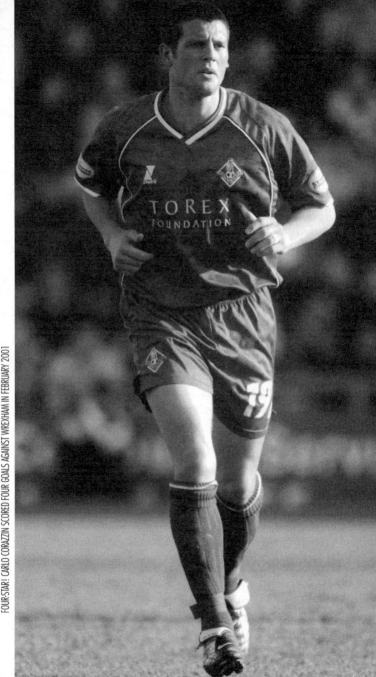

NORM WHO?

Mark Crossley's nickname was 'Big Norm' because of his likeness to Norman Whiteside, the former Manchester United and Northern Ireland star. When Mark was playing for Nottingham Forest his dad knew that he was making his debut for the club before 'Norm' did. The manager Brian Clough said that he "didn't want to worry the young keeper".

DODGIN THE MANAGER

When Norman Dodgin arrived at Boundary Park in July 1958 he introduced himself to one of the players with the immortal, "I'm Dodgin, the new manager." The player responded with, "So am I mate, you haven't seen him anywhere have you?"

ALL-TIME INTERNATIONAL TEAM

Given the ravages of time, different formations, rule changes, new balls etc. it would be almost impossible to put together a team of international players who have all represented Athletic and their countries at differing levels and agree that it would be the best. However, the following team based on a 4-4-2 formation would take some beating: Goalkeeper: Eddie Hopkinson; defenders: Denis Irwin, George Hardwick, Earl Barrett and Gunnar Halle; midfield: Bobby Johnstone, Mike Milligan, Bobby Collins and Jimmy McIlroy; forwards: Tommy Davis and Andy Ritchie; Substitutes: Andy Goram (goalkeeper); Richard Jobson (defender); Ronnie Blair (midfield); Andy Lochhead (forward); Supersub: David Fairclough (who else)?

I'M HAVING SOME OF THIS

A little known fact about Athletic's first ever Wembley appearance in the League Cup final is that one of the youth team players also stripped for the match. He came out with the team for the pre-match warm up, proceeded to kick about just like the rest of the squad, then he disappeared back to the dressing room. No-one 'in the know' noticed and the youngster got away with it scot-free.

CLUB CURFEWS

Athletic stayed on a fjord in Norway as part of the 1994/95 pre-season tour. It was the end of the trip and the players were allowed their customary one night out with a midnight curfew. A band played at the bar – a huge deck over the water, very picturesque with jazz music – while Lee Richardson, a seasoned drummer, was getting very agitated at the music and its lack of pace. The team asked the band if their drummer would like a rest and after their drinks break the players quietly slipped Lee in place in the middle of the band, complete with the flat cap he had pinched off the man he replaced. Without fuss, the band resumed playing – a typical jazz piece – and quickly the Latics drummer adjusted to the pace. However, after the first track and the realisation from the band that the boy could play, the jazz got spiced up and after a couple of speedier choruses a full drum roll broke out. The band dropped their music, the drummer played, the revellers all turned to see what was going on and the last comment heard was Joe Royle's: "I've paid 250 grand for a ******* drummer!" Laughs all round and Joe agreed to extend the curfew by an hour but they had to be back or a week's wages would be docked for latecomers. Sure enough a group of them returned around 12.45am to be met by Joe in the bar who bought them a drink and asked about the others and when they were returning. At this point an argument broke out about how you divide a half wit (Joe's name for Rick Holden that evening), and subsequently this became a quarter wit, eighth wit, etc. It was all to do with Rick's university education and Joe's university of life qualifications, and which were considered more relevant! The players and Joe went upstairs to bed but Joe sat on the landing with a candle, a book and a glass of wine awaiting the return of the late stragglers who thought they had got away with it. As they turned the staircase and walked the corridor, whispering and sniggering a voice would call out of the darkness, "a week's wages". Yes, Joe counted them in and he knew who was missing! No-one was sure how Steve Redmond got in that night but he can be thankful for quality Norwegian drainpipe manufacturing and correct fixings being used on the side of the hotel.

FA CUP SEMI-FINAL MISERY

Oldham Athletic hold the unenviable record of appearing in the most FA Cup semi-finals without actually progressing to the final! Their last two attempts have seen them be defeated by arch-rivals Manchester United.

HAVE BOOTS WILL TRAVEL

Athletic will have clocked up 10,088 miles after travelling away for the 2008/09 season. The season is a throwback to the Third Division (North) and South with the Latics being misplaced as the teams are predominantly southern-based. The only 'local' teams for League One encounters are Tranmere Rovers, Leeds United, Huddersfield Town and Stockport County. In an unprecedented year, the seven teams new to the division will all be based south of Birmingham. Charlton Athletic, Southampton and Norwich City dropped from the Championship while Brentford, Wycombe Wanderers, Exeter City and Gillingham were promoted from League Two. It means that a marathon will have to be endured for dedicated Latics fans with Stockport County being the shortest round-trip at 28 miles. Brighton will require a massive return trip of 546 miles.

ANGLO-SCOTTISH CUP 1978/79

The Anglo-Scottish Cup was entered for the first time by the Latics for the 1978/79 season. It kicked off with a home game against Sheffield United on August 5th which Athletic won 1-0 by a goal from Steve Taylor. Three days later another home game against Sunderland was victorious by 2-1 with Paul Heaton hitting the net twice. A trip to Bolton Wanderers on August 12th concluded the preliminary fixtures and a 0-0 draw was enough to see the Latics through. On September 13th, Athletic had to travel to Greenock Morton for a quarter-final and they were comprehensively beaten 3-0. The return leg at Boundary Park on September 26th was a completely different story. The Blues turned in an exemplary performance to overcome the visitors 4-0 and progress through to the semi-finals. Carl Valentine, Taylor, Alan Young and a Hayes own goal gave the Latics the victory. The semi-final draw paired Athletic with St. Mirren and the home leg on October 17th resulted in a 1-1 draw with Ian Wood scoring the Oldham goal. The away leg on October 31st resulted in another 1-1 stalemate. Young was on the scoresheet again and Oldham went through to the final on penalties. Burnley were the opposition and in the first leg at Boundary Park on December 5th, Young scored but it wasn't enough as the Clarets hit four. The second leg at Turf Moor on December 12th did bring success by 1-0 with Jim Steele scoring the only goal of the game, although Burnley won the tie with an aggregate score of 4-2.

IAN WOOD'S TESTIMONIAL

Oldham versus Kettering Town was the game played in aid of Ian Wood's testimonial on May 5th 1975. The Latics won by a score of 3-2 with goals from Maurice Whittle, Alan Groves and Gary Hoolickin. Also in the same month, the Latics made the short journey to Mossley to play a benefit game for Graham Schofield who had been forced to retire from the game after breaking his legs four times – ouch!

HELLO BRO

David Wilson was captain of the Athletic team that entertained Sheffield Wednesday at Boundary Park on December 24th 1910. When he took the toss for ends before the game, he faced his brother Andrew who was captain of the visitors. It was a rare occurrence for two brothers to captain First Division teams. The Latics won 1-0 and David Wilson later became manager of Oldham in the 1927/28 season.

ONE FOR ME – ONE FOR YOU

Athletic welcomed Manchester United to Boundary Park on October 6th 1923, in front of 15,120 supporters, in a match that marked the debut of Frank Hargreaves. It was a remarkable contest in which Sammy Wynne gave the visitors the lead through an own goal. But, he made amends with a penalty conversion on the half hour. Ten minutes into the second half, Billy Howson put Athletic ahead and on the hour mark, Wynne scored again to make it 3-1. However, Wynne got another own goal to become the only player to score two goals at each end in one match. The final score was 3-2 to Athletic.

FIVE POUNDS IS NOT MUCH

The Athletic chairman in 1962 was Harry Massey and he offered the players a £5 bonus per goal prior to the home game against Southport on Boxing Day. Little did he know that they were going to win the game by their highest-ever league score. The Latics pummelled Southport 11-0! Mr. Massey paid up but he learned his lesson and never offered the same deal again.

PLAY-OFFS 2006/07

Athletic entertained Blackpool in the first leg of the League One play-offs, the Latics' third venture into the lottery. John Sheridan had just taken over as boss at Boundary Park and this was his first season as full-time manager. The game was watched by 12,154 expectant supporters on May 13th 2007 but Blackpool were on an impressive run of seven consecutive wins and entered the fray as firm favourites. Andy Liddell got the only Latics goal in a 2-1 loss that gave Blackpool the advantage for the replay, played six days later at Bloomfield Road. The second game wasn't a fair match-up as the rampant Seasiders cruised into the Wembley final with a 3-1 win, their ninth successive victory. Matty Wolfenden scored the consolation goal for an under-par Athletic side and Blackpool went on to win the final, returning to level two of the Football League after a break of 28 years.

THE MARK OF ZORRO

During the 'big freeze' in the early 1960s, Latics chairman Harry Massey owned a building company which possessed an asphalt melter. Mr. Massey did not want to lose out to the inclement weather so he had the brainwave to make Boundary Park playable by burning off the ice with his melter. It looked a positively ingenious idea in January but when March arrived it was apparent that the idea had somewhat backfired. This was due to the fact that, as well as getting rid of ice, it did the same to grass, the result being that Harry's building sand replaced the lost grass for the latter third of the season and every time players slid into a tackle thereafter they burned their backsides! Opposing players and fans could easily recognise all the players on the Latics' books by the easily identifiable 'mark of Zorro' on their thighs.

FASTEST EVER GOAL

Athletic's fastest-ever goal was scored by Ian Robins on February 26th 1972. It was scored within five seconds of the game against Barnsley, which the Latics won 6-0. The game was also special for centre-half Dick Mulvaney as he netted his first goal for the club in a match which was a feast of attacking football.

OLDHAM ATHLETIC
Miscellany